Feathers
OF THE
Snow Angel
MEMORIES OF A CHILD IN EXILE

Rumpled sheets as white as snow, glittering in the light like snow-clad mountains. Warm soft feather bed enveloping my cold body, loving mother. It is no use; she is going to die.

From a small child's fragmented impression of snow, feathers and his mother's death comes the metaphor that pervades this harrowingly honest and poignant memoir — that of the snow angel.

The feathers of the snow angel wrapped the church. I shrank into nothing in its space. Do they imagine children do not suffer grief?

For the rest of his life Lionel Pearce struggled in the cold grief of the snow angel's embrace. The loss of his mother, the rejection by his mother's family and his eventual institutionalisation leave him damaged and vulnerable to feelings of self-pity, guilt, shame, worthlessness and fear.

In the tradition of *A Boy Called It* and *The Long Way Home* this memoir is distinguished by Pearce's courage in exposing his deepest emotions to the world and his rare ability to convey such emotional intensity in what is a work of both catharsis and brilliance.

Lionel Pearce was born at St Annes, Lancashire, in the United Kingdom in 1920. Following the death of his mother he was adopted at the age of five by a family in London, but at twelve he was sent as a child migrant to Fairbridge Farm in Western Australia. At fifteen he was working as a farm labourer, and then at nineteen, with the outbreak of war, he enlisted in the army and served in New Guinea.

After the war he successfully studied for university entrance and enrolled in medicine at Sydney University. He married in 1949 and he and his wife had five children. He worked as a teacher of zoology and botany until he retired in 1970 to pursue his love of music, art and writing.

Lionel Pearce died 13 May 2001.

Feathers OF THE Snow Angel

MEMORIES OF A CHILD IN EXILE

LIONEL PEARCE

FREMANTLE ARTS CENTRE PRESS

First published 2002 by
FREMANTLE ARTS CENTRE PRESS
25 Quarry Street, Fremantle
(PO Box 158, North Fremantle 6159)
Western Australia.
www.facp.iinet.net.au

Copyright © Lionel Pearce, 2002.

This book is copyright. Apart from any fair dealing for the purpose of private study, research, criticism or review, as permitted under the Copyright Act, no part may be reproduced by any process without written permission. Enquiries should be made to the publisher.

Consultant Editor Janet Blagg.
Production Coordinator Cate Sutherland.
Cover Designer Marion Duke.

Typeset by Fremantle Arts Centre Press
and printed by Success Print

National Library of Australia
Cataloguing-in-publication data

Pearce, Lionel, 1920–2001
Feathers of the snow angel

ISBN 1 86368 347 X.

1. Pearce, Lionel, 1920–2001. 2. Fairbridge Farm School (Pinjarra, W.A.) - Biography. 3. Immigrant children - Western Australia - Pinjarra - Biography. 4. World War, 1939–1945 - New Guinea - Personal narratives, Australian. I. Title.

304.8941042

The State of Western Australia has made an investment in this project through ArtsWA in association with the Lotteries Commission.

Prologue

The Snow Angel

Grandmother in your rocking chair before the fire. I wanted to tell you then I loved you, but shyness made me silent. Self-conscious, I sat on your knee and turned away from your expectant eyes. I was glad to escape from you onto the floor. I loved the soft creased leather of your black shoes and the roughness of your brown stockings, the gems of your rings and brooches whose pure melancholy colours whispered to me, the proud badges of a past exalted station. Your dignified white face set above your long black gown knew all about me. The flames played their gold tongues over your face and your eyes stared into the white-hot coals. I am you, Grandmother. If I had learned to know you, I would know myself by now. But you disappeared like a phantom and still you remain a phantom.

China washbasin and water jug decorated in pale blue sit like a monument on the marble top of the washstand, reach me through the iron bars of the cot. I see Mother tipping up the big beautifully shaped jug and letting hot water fall into the basin. I watch her bend over the basin and wash. I had upset the fragile lid of the soap container onto the hard marble top of the washstand and broken it, burdening myself with guilt, which was aroused whenever I gazed at the luxurious objects the washstand bore. Their shapes fascinated me. They were precious objects to Mother. The washstand and its treasure was now taboo. I was sure to break what I touched. I see them through the bars of the cot, the essentials of civilisation passed from generation to generation.

On the canal with Father. Green fields spread out on each side. I stand beside him watching in silence. Suddenly we come to a standstill in a lock made of massive wooden beams. Huge gates close behind us and the boat begins to sink past the sides of the lock. I feel my feet being taken from under me and see myself walled in. The boat goes down vertically very quickly, amidst a whirring of machinery and a swirling of water. I feel faint and clutch frantically at the rail. Father tells me to sit down on the seat. I see no more of the country as I cannot see over the rail and I am too shy to get up when I feel better.

The sea lies vast and smooth, engendering dreams of freedom from toil and want. The little tugs puffing huge billows of black smoke instil hope of escape from the duress of an unjust society. The liners drop over the horizon, their faint trails of smoke outlasting their departure. At the end of the pier on Sundays the tugs rest, their sterns low with coal. On the other side of the pier are the fishing boats, a web of ropes and wires lying mysteriously empty yet redolent of heroism and grief. The sea ever clutching at men to drag them down. The steam vessels thought they had conquered the great dumb sea. Men like showing off their supremacy over the sea, taking people for leisurely rides on their powerful boats over harbours, between villages and down canals.

I was playing on the floor. I could not learn how to play. The toys were cast offs. I could not fit them together. Even my father, folding up his long body, could not. The ill-matched toys baffled me and turned me to words which I could more easily copy down from the nursery rhyme book and which I proudly showed Mother. She was very pleased. We took the nursery rhyme book with us when she went sewing and I would sit precariously on a chair struggling to decipher the abstruse marks when she went upstairs in the big houses. Sometimes I went up with her and sat on the floor in the lady's lovely large room while Mother bent over the hem of her skirt. Mother seemed to have endless patience over obscure details of clothes.

I could not manipulate the slate pencil. It would skid on the smooth hard surface and put my teeth on edge with a terrible accusing screech. I used coloured pencils on paper starting with the capitals. The floor was my domain, especially under the table away from passing feet. I learnt the meaning of letters from the nursery rhymes she read to me.

I can construct again the walls and windows of the small house, a narrow yard at the back and a footpath in front. The snow would pile up against the door and below the windowsill. The snow bore the black figures of men. Only my mother preserved me although my father was kind when he came. My mother's family was my enemy. Mother stood between them and me. When she died they got rid of me.

How neatly everything fits together, the little houses, the concrete sea walls, the legs of the pier. It was a rare outing to go with a grown-up for a walk on the pier. The grown-up would be viewing his empire; the sea and I would be warmed and inflated with his satisfaction. He would treat me as an equal and I would search for his liners among the tramps. All was as it should be. The grey vainglorious houses with their imprisoned pot plants. The flagstones asleep in their positions. But all was dissolving, disappearing. I would look through the cracks of the pier. I hated anything to come between me and the sea, though I was taught to fear the sea where fishermen might drown on black howling nights. The soaking groynes shone like sleeping monsters. The waves fell over them washing their shiny sides. The flat sand was deserted. The sea wall seemed built to preserve its emptiness. The grey, bleak sky covered the sea, the formless sea. The flat sand under the uneven sea.

An unfathomable gulf of bitter self-knowledge after the war sought soothing in amusement, fairs. The black ferris wheel is going round in the sky. It is the tallest thing I have seen. I am afraid of it, I am afraid of all the fair. The machines threaten to make me part of themselves. I cannot understand the machines. Mother forgets me among all the people. I am a tiny thing among people's legs.

The men were deliberately trivialising life. Life is trivial. Only death is serious. This was the lesson the slaughter had taught them. But the soldiers treated us children seriously. The war had opened deeper the chasm between working men and women.

The black naked water was pulling me along, down the

river that flowed beneath the floor. I was bending over the edge of the hole in the floorboards, keeping my balance, watching the restless rapid black waves below. The wooden trapdoor lay beside me. A boy was with me looking down into the darkness too. We were both petrified with horror.

Our boat got out of the river into a whirlpool and the vortex was pulling it towards itself in spite of our prayers. Water was a nightmare to me, the threat of being totally engulfed. Yet the sight of its movement was irresistible.

A cowl was a horrible thing that suffocated babies. A cowl over one's head was supposed to be propitious. For me it was redolent of terrible punishments. A nightmare. It seemed the work of adults to instil children with fear. Fear of all that adults could do to them if they were disobedient. All the appurtenances of adult life were terrifying to children. Particularly horrifying were the tools of the law, the knife, the rope, the gun, the cell, the cat o' nine tails. A child is born into this mental torture chamber. How can he escape perennial fear?

Father's face as well as Mother's was beautiful. He would crouch down very small near the ground and turn his head with a smile that would overcome my timidity, so that I would climb on his back. His head was very large and heavy looking and his back very broad. He was always enveloped in dark, rough clothing. He would sometimes lift me onto his shoulders where I found the height terrifying and was unable to discover how to hang on, where to grasp him. I used to put my arms round his throat, throttling him in my fear of falling. He would gently put me down.

Father had a presence. He did not have to say anything.

The way he moved or remained still expressed gentleness and attention. He seemed to be thinking of a distant world.

Father was taboo, like all men in my mother's family. The old lady ruled in silence from a rocking chair. Her countenance turned me to stone so that I could not utter a word to my mother's mother. My mother's sisters treated me and Father like aliens. For them we existed in an inferior and diabolic world.

Father's countenance was often engrained with coal. He would look quite frightening. Yet he was very submissive to Mother and always deferred to her wishes. He was like her child although Mother was only a tiny thing. I pretended to side with Mother and repressed my affection for him.

Father could not stay because Mother was living with her sisters. He seemed so big in that tiny house, especially standing before the door under the low steep roof. Father had arguments with my mother's elder sister, who was a strict unforgiving person with a grotesquely long thin neck, which was always encircled by a stiff black collar. She had the face of an avenging angel and never relaxed her disapproval of my existence.

My father loved the water and when he took me out he usually took me on a boat, either a ferry or a canal boat. We were both shy and silent and we accompanied each other like twins activated in unison by some unseen bond. Although self-conscious, I was never afraid of him and he was never irritated by me, clumsy though I was, for as a boy of four I was barely able to keep my feet and although Mother had taught me to read and write, I could understand nothing that was said to me.

I have the conviction that Father was a soldier who had recently returned from the war, or who, having returned, had met hard times, for he still wore his long greatcoat against whose coarse wool I can still feel my cheek pressing as I walked between him and Mother after an evening at the fair in the long twilight of summer. And yet, in my memory his face is young. My father was a miner. The mines were our earthy and only gods. Coal was the lifeblood of the people. They literally loved coal and it was their great joy and the justification of their existence to see the black smoke billowing from the tugs as they set out to sea or to watch the faint grey trails of liners crossing the horizon.

My father was fond of shows and fairs and used to enjoy going round the booths in the pier pavilion and the sideshows in the fairs. He was a good marksman at the coconut shies and after a win would break open the coconut, throw back his head and drink the milk and hand me a piece to munch while I followed him and Mother round the turbulent grounds. He was probably one of the few heroes back from France, like walking statues in their long greatcoats, followed wherever they went by the admiration of little boys who would crowd round them, attention riveted on their every movement. There was boldness and authority in their movements which promised a new freedom and strength and a new world of self-reliant men and women. The old subservient shrinking had gone. But though they might no longer lift their caps to the boss, they were still the slaves of women, high or low.

Father was never home. The house belonged solely to women apart from his rare visits when he would sit with his cap in his hand on the couch, listening complacently to Mother.

He was at home in the mine and once he took us to the

pithead, ushered us in the tiny cage and lowered us down into the mine. I wanted to stay down there but we soon had to return because Mother was uneasy in the unearthly world underground. Above ground he proudly provided us with afternoon tea in the miners' canteen.

We used to go home after the fair and eat fish and chips in front of the fire. Father would come in and sit in silence while Mother spread out my parcel of chips on the table; the smell and taste of vinegar and salt was delicious.

I remember him sitting on the couch, his cap in his hand, head down, looking at the floor. He seemed listless, exhausted. Mother was speaking to him in a reproving way. He listened deferentially. It must have been Christmas, for he had given me some new expensive looking toy soldiers, for which Mother upbraided him. I said I liked my old ones best to please her. I felt he was wounded.

My father must have found it difficult to understand my fear of falling although he gave no sign that he found it unusual, behaving as though nothing had happened even though I might be trembling with terror. When he visited us I could see how shy and afraid of Mother he was. I always took Mother's side, which seemed to intensify his loneliness, confirm his isolation. His generous gifts I accepted coldly as if they were my right, secure in Mother's love.

The large gaps between the planks of the pier show the sea below, a green inscrutable mask. I carefully step over them, held by Father and Uncle. They converse in low tones, their eyes held on the distance, alert for a ship on the horizon. The sea was indisputably their domain, the liners and tugs their charges. They held my hand firmly.

The men were always in black suits. They were always long and bony. They were always cold, rubbing their hands or thrashing their sides. Their eyes were always far away.

On the small deal table in the cold bare kitchen behind the sitting room, Mother would cut up the fruit for the mince pies for Christmas. She would roll out the dough for the pastry, leaning all her weight on the rolling pin's handles, her white strong arms bare. Each little pan of the pastry tin was carefully filled. She would give me the mixing bowl to lick out. Sitting on the floor, I scoured it with my finger. I helped her wash up, standing on a chair, and attempted to get a shine on the stove with the blacking brush. On Christmas morning before we all sat down to eat she gave me a mince pie as a reward for helping. At Christmas time the table in the sitting room was made twice as long. It was beautifully laid and decorated with holly and big crackers. Mother seemed to do everything. Soon the room was full of people: aunts, uncles, cousins. We children were rewarded for our homage to the Christmas tree and took our presents to the floor. At the long tightly packed table the yearly delicacies were savoured — the stuffing, the pudding, the nuts and raisins. The thin slice of year old pudding revealed the glint of sixpences. How we were shamelessly devoted to things. We forgot one another in our toys and food. There was always jealousy over toys; for me there was always depression, for I could not manage toys. How gentle and serious the black clad men were but their minds were far away. How practical the women were. The world we lived in was made by women

A thick slice of stale white bread, the crust cut off, was cut into cubes, put in a basin and covered with warm milk and sugar for my tea. This was delicious, like the warmth and light of the fire and the smell of coal. The fire seemed never to go out. A heavy iron round-walled pot and a big iron kettle were constantly on the boil; the fire was also used for heating irons. I remember the fragrance and dazzling whiteness of washing being dampened, folded and ironed, the hissing steam billowing up to the ceiling, before it was stacked in resonant cane baskets.

The wallpaper was patterned with colours, beautiful pictures, repeated unendingly. The sun-like mantle of the gaslight threw its beams half over the walls, so that one had to dive for the colours in the shadowy corners, repeating the fleeting capture of the flowers and leaves. Time passed as my tendrils clasped these flowers, as I lay in my cot in the light of dawn or night.

There is doubt that they will recognise me as human. Perhaps I do not want to be one of them and want to destroy what is called human. One wants to be both human and not human, to be both god-like and animal-like. This starts very early when one hates and loves the people about one.

Crossing cautiously the gaps between the beams, I wandered the piers. They were less cold than the snow covered streets. The movement of the water hypnotised me and I hung onto the rail lest I should stumble against the edge and sink beneath the invincible arms of the sea. In spite of my horror of the sinister chambers of the deep, curiosity led me onto the boats and buildings round the end of the pier.

The sighing of waves on the sand. The tang of wind blowing over discarded seaweed. The distant smoke. All in a synthesis of motion, a single experience. This made home. The little black tugs, so empty inside, whose volumes of black smoke on the horizon often fool you into expecting a romantic liner, were tied up at the end of the pier. Beside them the cluttered fishing boats waited, abandoned all day. The sea was ceaselessly agitated and so were the dark figures of heavily clad men. Castles of coal rose in the broad sterns of the tugs, pressing them down into the water. Their prows leapt out. Everything was waiting for the proper moment to act. I was too early or too late. The Irish Sea, pregnant with sadness, stretched out before me like an infinite page.

The long piers stretch out into the grey sea towards the horizon, a fine line, far, far away. A carpet of snow on the footpath melts into slush, which soaks my shoes and freezes my feet. The shiny boughs of trees burst magically into leaf. Throngs of people brush their heavy coats together looking for enjoyment, breathing smoke, rubbing their hands together or keeping them deep in their pockets. There is ceaseless repartee and low laughter. Mother drags me through the forest of limbs.

Walking home in the gloaming while the silent gaslighter does the rounds on his bicycle, lighting the street lamps with a magical strike of his long pole. The large yellow lanterns shed a warmth in the dusk. Instinctively I find my way home to the cluttered room in the low, gardenless house where everyone is too busy to notice me. An incessant activity continues above my head in a room whose only impression on me is the enigma of people's legs making purposeful journeys across the room. Before the fragrant burning coal with its blue curls and incandescent face hangs the washing on the opened out clothes horse. The room is cold. Washing is everywhere.

Grandmother seems inseparable from the high-backed

rocking chair, knitting in the rug of her lap between dry, brown, creased hands. Hands lying like reflections of her face. I crawl beneath the feet of busy determined women, looking up into their inclined, emaciated, worried faces. They do not talk to me. I am in their way. Underneath Grandmother's long black skirt, her chair rocks unceasingly. Her soft, black, leather shoes remain together on the carpet, timeless and worn. Her black stockings are warm. Grandmother and the fire, permanent occupants of the room, both working to the same end.

My mother was a slight, small, girlish figure dominated by the other women in the house. She and I would go down alone over the sea wall where she sat near the edge of the sea, perfectly still and quiet, while I with a tin bucket and wooden spade stumbled in the sand about her. The sand was empty and the vacant sea stretched far away to the broad horizon. We were both lonely and frightened. My mother was frightened of well-dressed men and when a gentleman walked along the water's edge she would call me sharply to her, although I wanted to respond to his smile. I was ashamed of our unfriendliness.

The texture of the golden sand attracted me but I was unable to compact it together into sand pies, in spite of my deliberate patting. My mother never turned to help me. I strayed from her along the solitary beach to the old pier whose gigantic columns filled me with wonder. I caressed their smooth, bleached surfaces. The distance of the pier's incursion over the sea intrigued me. How the pillars stood in the fathomless sea baffled me.

A man will do anything for the love of a woman. He will reduce himself to the most pitiful state of dependence, the most ludicrous state of servility. He will commit all sorts of crimes. By man, I mean the man throughout his life, beginning with the love of his mother and ending with the love of his last wife or mistress. If the love of his mother is not quickly transformed into the love of his wife he will persecute the whole world for her loss all his life long. Love of his mother fills him with contempt for other men, no matter what their age. He will do everything he can to belittle and destroy them in her eyes. He is the instrument of blind passion all his life. Yet, strangely enough, he will become the slave of other men to please her, however shallow such a course may be and however self-destructive. He will abandon her to please her.

Search the flat grey sea. The smoke of ships on the horizon arrests our eyes and takes us on journeys away from the circle we cannot cross, of work and poverty. The black forbidding groynes stretch far out into the sea one after another, covered in slippery coats of drenched seaweed but some men undaunted go out on them in great mackintoshes to fish, tempting the unpredictable waves.

The long thin neck of Aunty terrified me. Thin necks were a sign of something sinister, a sign to be wary of. Her tight black dress and hat were immaculate and threatening. She disliked me as something alien to her world. She never knew where to put me. She could not sympathise with my clumsiness and stupidity. She was a black divinity, intelligent, superior, supernatural. My uncle was her chief creation, a chubby, submissive, happy man, who always stood up for me. She could not reconcile herself to the terrible straits Mother and I were in: illegitimate child and unmarried mother. She had no children. We were outcasts, whom she could materially assist but never socially reinstate. Mother retreated into her work, endless washing, ironing, sewing and cooking. I clung to her and was happy helping her. She had a sewing machine, in a wonderful box. When she leaned over the material she would let me turn its handle. I turned it with both hands as fast as I could. I would please her by going faster and faster.

Rumpled sheets as white as snow, glittering in the light like snow-clad mountains. Warm soft feather bed enveloping my cold body, loving mother. It is no use; she is going to die. Blue flowered walls. Musical brass bed and hard iron cot, like a cage. Shining brass knobs. Mother's voluminous bedclothes and long white bolster. Smelly cot. Flashing white sheets rumpled. Soft golden warm skin of Mother, dressing, washing, bent at the cold marble washstand. Graceful back. Tight clothing. White lace bonnet, tied with tapes under her chin, shining in golden gaslight. Mother tying tapes with small adroit hands, quick, efficient, framing her face like Grandmother. People are what their mothers are, also what their mothers are not.

Iron tub, dull grey, cold, containing a sea of warmth under the glare of the burning coal. Fragrance of coal, white face, warmer than the sun, hotter. Surrender to fire, to caressing warm water. Sponge in Mother's hand making warm rivers, red carbolic soap. Pink dentifrice. The subject of detailed care by Mother, against everyone else's indifference.

Dollies in pretty check dresses, a farthing each, for washing. Running errands to the rich cave of the corner shop for Mother. Wooden washing board. Mother bent over, rubbing sheets. Sleeves rolled up, wringing sheets. Long yellow soap bars.

Coal man, a sack over his head, back bent under the

wet bag of coal, returning silent with empty bag. Shouting 'coal' in the street. Getting coal from the coal shed, searching for the biggest pieces to please Mother; beautiful stone, black jewels, free shapes, a beautiful and useful thing. Coal is alive. It sleeps then burns, then collapses. Coal smoke is a good smell; a coal's face is shiny like Mother's. Coal is white hot inside and tells the future if you can read it.

There was a crowd of wooden legs supporting the pier which reached out over the sea like a bridge, inviting me to a promised land. He would take me there, the black clad figure of Father, or Uncle. My hand in his, I would step hesitantly across the spaces through which the green water beckoned far below. How small these giants made me feel and how fond of them they made me with their kindness.

I went among the smooth rigid columns of the pier as though they were spellbound giants, only awaiting my coming to begin a horrifying feast. Their bodies were hard, too hard for a human body. I absorbed their volumes.

He loitered under the pier, the ubiquitous evil stranger. If he saw you, you were caught because he fascinated you. His black form and mien engulfed you like a storm and his knowing smile petrified you.

Avoiding the cold waves, I walked to where the tiny figure of Mother sat on the sand a few yards from the ocean. How alone we two were. The only figures on the beach, the empty sea and deserted pier lying before us. The grey sea wall behind us, over which the sea charged in winter. She must have felt me as a burden, handicapped by my shyness and awkwardness. Because of me she was ostracised and pitied by her family.

Mother was always absorbed in her work or in unknown thoughts that arose while she was working. She would take sewing down to the beach. She was never idle. She paid no attention to what I was doing. I could not get things to work. The sand would not stick. She sat on with bent head, never seeming to notice my frustration.

Mother taking off her black dress and bending over the washbasin. I cannot undo the locks of the cot, so I climb up on its edge and fall on the floor. The hardness of the floor shocks me. My own screams terrify me. I sink into something soft and anaesthetic. Behind the black iron bars of my cot shine the golden sentinels of Mother's bed and the blazing white of her sheets and bolster. My cot was a rattling and smelly pit where I was caged. Only golliwog consoled me while I was confined in it.

The wood of the copper lid was white like driftwood. It fitted the copper perfectly, pealing a single organ note as it was put down. The copper was a stone belly full of white entrails completed by the lid. Steam escaped, covering Mother's face with dew. I was fond of wooden things: the corrugated washboard's series of identical waves, the solid walls of the troughs bearing deep lakes of blue and white water. The copper was a rare square rock with a scorching fire. The tubs contained seas. My mother seemed bound to them. Impatiently I pulled her away, but the grey walls of the laundry cell imprisoned her while she rinsed clothes and dissolved blue bags. Her arms bare, she wrung the clothes with her hands, then she stretched to reach the line and never ceased holding up her arms, calling impatiently for pegs which I picked up off the ground. She stretched out her hand without looking down and took them from my hand. On cold mornings the sheets hung stiffly on the line and Mother had to wrestle with them to get them off the line and inside in front of the fire.

The scissors grinder and the tinker pushed, with bended back, their fragile wooden carts up the hill. I would run out with scissors and kettle and watch in wonder as these silent ascetics made them new. The little coalman pushed his cart laden with coal. He was all black, the embodiment of unflagging superhuman effort. Bent under a grimy sack of coal, he went through the rooms of the house unseeing, taciturn, and returned, the sack empty over his shoulder.

Mother was part of nature. The universe spoke to me through her. She was always working for others. I learnt from her to work for others, to please others at any cost to myself. In that way we get absolution for our sin and calm our sleepless guilt. Mother battled through the snow with me at her side, my hand in hers, stopping me from falling. She would wipe the blinding snow from my eyes. Mother was very small like me. She was always smartly dressed. We would hurry past the iron spikes of the rich houses, their flights of stone steps and heavy doors. We never passed another soul. The rich would not forsake their cosy rooms in such weather. I sometimes went into those high spacious rooms, with beautifully clean floors, to play with the rich children, coveting and assuming possession of their beautiful toys. I saw the rich children as fair game to be robbed and repulsed. Mother had to protect them from me to keep on the right side with her employer. She was just, and opposed to disorder. She projected harmony about her, always putting things to rights. People liked this and used her, allowing her to look after their needs, to wear herself out for them. She looked after her own family as well, doing all the cooking and washing. There seemed to be very few men left in the world. They were only visitors. One was Father. They seemed to come from another land. They had more important things on their mind than home. They were always very kind but restless and eager to be off. Everybody suffered from cold and insufficient food.

I have always been homeless. My mother and I were put outside the pale of the family for our contempt of family morality, a morality sanctified by religion. The big black shapes floating in and out of our house were probably priests. They engulfed such outcasts as us in their black compassionate bellies. I see them like a macabre dance, forbidding and stunting all embryonic freedom, making impossible any release from the chains of guilt put on us by the family.

I wanted to help my mother. She would lift me up on a chair so I could try to wash up. I would hang round her when she was washing in the back yard and go round to the store for soap and dollies of blue. The store was a friendly warm place, up two giant steps, with inexhaustible things hanging everywhere and air thick with mysterious smells. A wide slab of scoured wood was the counter and a kind old man gave rewards of liquorice and sweets.

Oil. Vinegar. Salt. Newspaper. Chips. The purring yellow gaslight. Warm sunless twilight.

Machine. Mother's machine. Lace curtains. White lace.

Men moving you around with god-like authority. Fear of their punishment making you surrender.

Station platform beside Mother, tongue-tied. Sooty black engine half full of coal, streaming with rain. Black wet grit. Open red furnace fed by pendulum shovel, swollen with coal.
   Low icy sky. Compressed snowflakes. Inescapable cold.
   Coiled sleeping dragon sea. Land of the sea taboo to children.
   Black smoke for a tug, the grey smoke a liner. The eternal drama of the sea; ships of dreams, denizens of the waves.
   Slush. Cold, snow, water and mud. Ever drizzling. Hard cold pavements. The sea springing up over the wall. Searching for her to take the heavy heart.
   The grey facades of immemorial apartments, rejecting. Spacious hall and wide staircase. Kitchen, harbour from the cold.
   Breathless hush of snow, pure white. Walking, walking long straight treeless streets. All the same grey facades staring defiantly at the sea. Scurrying by to escape judgement. The drawing room. Mother kneeling at the hem of the lady's dress, inserting pins. I play on the carpet.
   My mother was always impatiently sewing, doubled up over material rapidly falling off the table. The wheels of the machine had a magnetic attraction for me and I strained my hardest to turn the handle as fast as I could.

The fireplace was a perpetual danger because the chimney with its thick pelt of soot could so easily catch fire. There were stories of little boys sent up chimneys to clean them out and I was eager to go up ours. But the sweep would come, a black little man with a white face, a bunch of long sticks on his shoulder, a circular broom on the end of one.
   The gaslight purred over the middle of the table, round

which we stood while its mantle grew incandescent. A white tablecloth was on the table. We unwrapped our warm bundles of fish and chips, pressing the creases out of the newspaper. I had my own small bundle of chips. My cot was waiting in the darkness of the other room. I longed for Mother to put me in it, to kiss me and abandon me to sleep beside her big bed.

The fish shop over the road was full of yellow light. You could see the bent figures twirling about in it. The big saltcellar and the large bottle of vinegar were turned upside down, one after another, every few minutes, and a heavily mantled figure dropped deftly out of the familiar shop and hurried away. The odour of vinegar and oil hung in the warm air of the cosy shop. The owner and his wife, with large florid faces, were the friends of everybody. How small I was among the giant figures pressed against the counter. How important I felt among them.

Mother was small like me. She recognised her betters and depended on them, rather than men of her own class. They saw she was kept busy. In winter, the room was humid with drying clothing. The clothes horse was burdened with folded and mangled sheets. White steam rose from the hissing iron. The fragrance of cotton filled the room. My mother rescued me from the angry aunts who found me stupid and reproached her for it. My mother and I are not wanted.

I damaged the delicate mantle of the gaslight on the mantelpiece with my inquisitive fingers. Everyone wonders how the mantle could have been damaged. I suppress the temptation to confess, fearing the exacerbation of my already probationary state. Self-tortured, I stare up at the fruitless efforts of the adults to make the mantle work. Someone has to go out for another one and my prison walls recede. How the chalk-perforated walls of the fairy light become incandescent amazes me. One is born, a timid primitive into a long woven world that you can decipher only with patient teaching. Otherwise you are condemned to permanent childhood. The withdrawing of love is permanent punishment. Without love there is no teaching, no explanation. The women surrounding me punished me with their tight-lipped disapproval. I was afraid of this more than physical violence.

I could not write letters with my slate pencil. It slipped sideways leaving white trails on the clean grey surface. I had to conceal that my slate was broken after my stepping on it, so as not to suffer another loss of love. I did not know what to do with the lead soldiers either. I liked natural things, like the snow piled up on the footpath outside the house and the snowflakes finding their tortuous way down in front of the frosted windowpane. The whiteness of the snow was vast and beautiful, like the greyness of the sea and the greenness of new leaves.

I clung to the unbearable, mysterious heat that enveloped my body as I lay in bed with scarlet fever. The heat delineated me as a body for the first time. Unable to understand what threatened my existence, I clutched at even the severest misery for the sense of life it gave me. My mother sank beside me with a basin of cold water and caressed me. She seemed angry that no one had bathed my face. She was in a hurry to return to work.

The silent music of the snow. A thousand prying fingers suffocating. Mother radiating warmth, dragging a child through the snow. Stiff, leafless sticks. Ice air. Vista of rain drenched streets. After Mother died, I was compelled by hunger to become a scavenger for coppers, farthings, ha'pennies and pennies, glad to survive on a pittance, like all the working-class after the war. Intense cold sterilising everything. Vain hunt for Mother. Begging for pennies.

When people are undressed before one another what will they do? Beauty is the form of Mother, the concrete experience of love. I wanted to see the naked body of Mother doing things. This action is the content of my love for Mother's body, the raw material of love. Sex is a joke in the middle-class world. Of love it has no comprehension because it does not understand the role of beauty or the source of it, in the freedom of a woman's body.

Only the working people understand the beauty of the body because it lies in their fruitful movements.

The inert form of death is no longer the person. Movement has vanished. Memory is movement that will vanish.

Sea front always accepting — widows, unwanted children, returned soldiers; young women flaunting their unexpected wealth, successful dark clad smart small men, big men idle in rags, ill-treated horses, pampered dogs. Giant piers dwarfing, taking possession of the sea, endless roads over the sea to the empty horizon. Ceaseless expanding activity without cause or goal. Over the menacing waves I stand on the rock-like platform of the pier. I walk out over the sea.

A big stout man is up on a dray thrashing a horse. I

want to thrash him. He knows. Although rankling under the injustice and cruelty, I would rather let him thrash the horse than thrash me. Cowardice, before the threat of physical violence in his eyes. An animal cannot pretend. My fear quells my hatred. I had become his accomplice and guiltily subdued my feelings.

Sand, golden, wet, falling apart. The unsubdued sea. The heart of man cannot take orders without becoming a rebel. Infinitely divisible sand. Water over one's feet. The jungle of man. The tremendous haven of the Irish Sea, slumbering dreaming, fathomless love and grief.

I sit on the floor looking up at Mother's face concentrated on rolling out the dough. Back and forth her whole body moves over the table. The sleeves of her blouse rolled up. She is always in a hurry. There seems no end to her work. I am down on the floor painstakingly licking clean an empty mixing bowl. The smell of baking pastry and raspberry jam fill the kitchen.

I am going down by myself onto the sand, which is soft between my toes. My bare feet sink, and I stumble. Our house is just across the narrow road beside the sea. A row of fishing boats lie on the sand a long way from the water. All kinds of tackle form enigmatic webs in their sterns. An old man is sitting on the sand on a kitchen chair moving a long net through his hands. Suspiciously, he asks me where I live. I show him where my home is. He tells me sharply to go home. A woman descends from his boat, talks to me kindly and invites me to take a sweet from a bottle. I am reassured. I linger near the man, mesmerised by the endless folds of the net on the sand but he commands me to go again with hostility. I feel rejected by these people who I like and want to stay with. They are raggedly dressed and their faces are tanned and bony. I want them to take me with them at night out to sea, so I can help them fishing.

One night there is a terrible storm. The night is pitch black. I thought about the fishermen. Later I was told one of the boats did not return.

Green engine, barely tamed explosion, impatient at the empty platform, your magically round wheels working miracles of motion. Kind and cruel, the train following lamely behind hills of coal thrown into the flames of your mouth. Come away from the edge. You'll be sucked under. I run over the platform shocked by its hard surface. Conjure happiness, excitement, hope, promise, sand, salt, smiles, images of the train, crudely drawn a thousand times. I am Mother, her tiny black form and flushed face in command of the whole journey. Crossing points, throwing away unwanted rails. Our train realises our decision, purpose. I exalt in the flight of earth behind me. One is pulled through an experience, like birth, to find oneself living anew, living again. After a journey one starts living again.

I have new shoes, which slip, carry my feet from under me. They pinch my toes. I hobble along behind a loveless group of women at the seaside, containing my misery. A stranger, my aunt, has become my mother. She only cares about her female friends who are laughing together as they walk along the narrow road beside the sea and the line of pretty cottages. They are too happy to notice me. Aunt tells me to play on the sand and that I know where the house is as I have been there before. I do not remember being here before. Will I get lost? They have seduced my aunt-mother away from me, those frivolous friends of hers. I will let the water cover me against the sea wall. It is slowly stepping in. Puddles appear behind me. Soon the whole sea will rise over my head and I will not be able to escape. Panic grips me. I find an escape route around the puddles over the wet sand. I will get my new shoes wet. I take my socks and shoes off.

My fingers pinched Mother's cheek. I did not recognise death. She did not wake up. Her face was like a stranger's, emaciated, expressionless, bloodless. I coveted the pennies that lay on her eyes. They seemed to be lying there for children to pick up. I greedily took one, imagining changing it in the high street for a bag of stale cakes or a parcel of hot chips. A woman working in the room told me to put it back. I was very puzzled. I could not understand why the body of Mother was so unrelentingly silent and still. I did not know what death was. She was still a resident of the house, lying alongside of others going busily here and there. The working woman seemed to be cleaning up the house. No one was looking after me. I was waiting only to get outside where I might get something to eat. Later, relatives came dressed in their best clothes. Milling around busily they took no notice of me, although someone had dressed me up in a new suit. There was a lot of talking. Then there came into the house those who always manage everything, big men in dark clothes. They always know what to do and everybody stands aside and watches them. They were carrying Mother out in a long box. I tried to stop them, hanging on to the side of the box grimly until I was pulled away. Then they all moved out among black horses, carriages. Everything was glossy: the horses, the clothes and coaches, a grand ceremony outside the low cottage.

The feathers of the snow angel wrapped the church. I shrank into nothing in its space. Do they imagine children do not suffer grief? Big beams pondered overhead. How small and non-existent I was, sitting in the hard pew like a lost seed. All Mother's relatives were strangers, even enemies to me, yet they brought me with them as though we were not forever separate. The snow covered the ground. Cold air weighed on the snow. The black figures drove me like someone accidentally left behind. I searched among them for Mother's face.

We formed ranks on the side of the grave all in black. The silence and cold were intense. We were all shuffled together by death around his shrine in the earth; unresisting, dumb, stupefied black figures, white faces sulking. I felt very small among the towering, heavy adults, all lowering on the ground. My aunts and uncles guarded me on each side with severe stares. There was an enormous hole in front of me full of darkness and on the far side the big man in a long white dress, who had talked incomprehensibly in the church, was reading from a small book. Two men picked up the long polished box I had seen them carry Mother out of the house in and, with ropes, lowered it hand over hand into the hole, without remonstrance from the spellbound onlookers. No one lifted a finger to stop them although they were putting my mother into a hole. The men's arms kept letting out the rope. Then they began to put earth into the hole. Still everybody watched without stirring. I wanted to laugh and cry. A stifled giggle escaped my lips. An aunt heard me and gave a freezing stare. I writhed with shame and guilt but still could hardly suppress my need to laugh and cry. I knew my mother was not in that hole. That she was somewhere walking around. I just had to find her again.

I stood between my black aunts listening. A single bell kept ringing. The awful gaping hole with the earth waiting beside it. Leaving the cemetery unwanted with Mother's family. Father was too poor. They kept the silence of the snow and guided me along with their black coats.

I went to stay with my fearful aunt. I wandered along the streets and hung around the piers, blackness in my heart, my senses open to every despairing impression. Entreating the grey walls of the wealthy to relinquish my mother, to excuse her from her sewing, to let me have her back.

The long thin neck of Aunty terrified me, dressed in a tight black dress; the severity of her face and accusing look turned me into an outcast. Watching the pictures, reading novels, people are forgetting their painful lives.

The ocean flung itself up the rocks and the waves drove up the cliffs to overtake me as I crept down. Bravado and fear struggled with each other. I craved the excitement of the massive waves' destruction but wanted to reach the sand, dreading that the hungry sea would carry me off the furrowed brow of the cliff. I ran back and stole forward. Like forked lightning, the breaking waves ran up the black chiselled rocks towards me.

Once in the safety of the house, the fury of the waves grew and water pelted the windows like stones and spread like molten metal under the door. I burrowed down in bed inside the drum of the beating ocean, soaking my coarse linen pillow with tears. Aunty called me to her bed.

There are two women walking together by the sea below. I am too shy to approach. Aunty and her companion are talking. I run down to the sand and trail behind. They forget me. I become used to being alone. I learn that I am small, awkward, unwanted.

The snowflakes dancing before the windowpane kept me inside for the third day. I had got used to haunting the streets, begging for coppers and scavenging for food. I felt oppressed by confinement indoors and disillusioned with the old broken toys left on the cold floor. I had lost Mother. In spite of my long wanderings in the streets, I could not find her. A young man in working clothes burst through the room carrying a long-handled shovel. He was going to clear the snow away from the front door. He spoke roughly to a woman cleaning the house, ordering her not to let me go out. He threatened me with a bashing if I did. I had never been spoken to like this before and was terrified of him. Wiping the windowpane, I saw the snow nearly up to the windowsill. I could not see far through the jostling mass of snowflakes, each white figure dancing without hindrance in the air. They seemed to occupy the whole world.

Uncle rides a penny farthing bicycle, my aunt said to me. I disbelieved her but on going outside, I saw it leaning against the white wall. Later I saw his plump figure balancing on it in the street. He seemed to exercise a mysterious force that held his fat little body above the ground. Uncle was a cheerful man, appeasing the severity of my aunt. Her sharp face and thin body judged me guilty of every imaginable crime and threatened horrible punishment, while my uncle's genial smile and corpulent body always provided welcome escape. My mother had taught me to look after myself, so I had only to present myself for meals and bed. During the day I wandered around the streets looking for Mother. No one mentioned her death.

The grey residentials rose all alike beside one another in their common respectability. There was always a step down into the street and fine ladies came down in their tight black bodices and swirling skirts. I had often waited in these houses while my mother did their sewing, a silent visitor for the aspidistras, my book of nursery rhymes open on my knees. Sometimes Mother took me into the warm friendly kitchen under the stairs, where the maids and cook all sat around the kitchen table chatting and laughing.

A working man sat in a box in the narrow entrance of the vast pavilion at the end of the pier and indifferently took my ha'penny to enter. His dour silence and old worn clothing signified both the freedom and the tyranny of my class to me and I passed by him with a mixture of delight and terror, feeling very small. He did not betray any understanding of what a treat he was giving me. His mechanical gestures hinted at annoyance. His eyes seemed to expect an adult above me, to shepherd me through the snares of his enormous snail-like house.

I had cadged money to get in. With trepidation and shame I would run besides the swirling skirts of a soldier's greatcoat until the deeply cut face of a possessed soul would lean over me to listen seriously to my argument. Then the puissant arm of the hungry working man would plunge deep into his clothing and return with an envied collection of coins, from which he would peremptorily hand me a penny and stride on. Shamefaced I walk away in the opposite direction.

The amusement pavilion became an obsession, an escape from grief. An urgent desire to get in would suddenly possess me and conquer my timidity, making me beg and face the old man at the entrance, impatient to exchange my loneliness for the glitter of each of its tiny stalls.

I was used to Mother's absences. I thought her death only another absence from which I never stopped expecting her to return. I did not understand why I was standing stiffly with all these unknown people with solemn faces around a long rectangular hole into which the box containing Mother was being put. It was all so irrational, to put a person in a box in a hole. I could not restrain my giggling in spite of the murderous glare from Aunty and the looks of incredulity from kinder faces. I sank deep into guilt. I had committed some unnameable crime. No one explained Mother's disappearance to me. An endless search for her began. Her family was punishing me with her disappearance. I felt I was the culprit. Life does not go on forever yet we go on living every day as though it does.

Cold. Snow robbing the sight. A window with no world. Strange caretakers in the house. A dour woman cleaning. A big man striding through the house grumbling. I wanted to go out to scavenge something to eat and to go on with my search for Mother, to wait in front of the houses where she might be working. I was not to go out he told the woman angrily. With a long-handled shovel, he hastened through the room to clear the snow from the front door. If you go out I'll bash your head in. She compliant; I cringing on the floor fumbling with toys, looking out for the snow to stop.

The big men in long black overcoats with soft white faces towered over us, my two aunts on kitchen chairs with their backs to the end of the table and myself in my best clothes, standing bewildered between their knees. They were the giants who know. We listened to them to learn the truth, to do what they said we should do. They were kind and terrible. They said I would like it in London where I would find opportunities and a good education. My aunts agreed. Men don't realise they are incapable of educating. Mother had already fully educated me. I didn't want to leave home but would agree to please them, promising myself I would return one day. I was not one to take opportunities but my brain was infused with vague shadows of great adventures, so sacrificing my love of home and Mother, I agreed to go with them. They put me in a tomb full of tendering shades where my mother and home could never come.

Yet I thought, when consenting, that I was deliberately consenting and that I would go back. I yielded to them to please them, in fear of them, to please my aunts, to please the all powerful adults. When I had appeased their wishes, I would return and find Mother. I was cunning, I thought. I was Mother's not theirs. But I never returned. Thus children are beguiled from their homes and relatives by minions of church or state, exhorted by fear of displeasing, by the need for adults' love and protection. They go heartbroken but unprotesting into exile.

When I got to the institution, sitting between the two black-coated giants in the front seat of their car, tea was over. I was given my egg and bread and butter on a table by myself, assuring the nun I had been taught by my mother how to eat an egg. At the far end of the huge room a ring of cheeky inquisitive faces sat around a table. They threatened to take my place in the attention of grown ups. I hated their confident appropriation of privilege. I hated their happiness in their assurance of loyalty. Their group was a single being on which would be lavished the love that until then I had possessed alone. I refused to join them. I hated the group, the round table, the polished grinning masks. They were mostly smaller than me, and later, when I could not avoid mixing with them, I began to bully them.

To children, human beings are the form of their dress. I was horrified by the massive forms of the sisters in their broad ankle-length gowns, whose colour brown has always repelled me. Their massive involved headdress terrified me. It seemed to go back and forth like the pinions of some watchful bird. These huge creatures engulfed me away from Mother. They could not console me. I despised the mob of children. The whole building was like a mountain tomb whose walls were tiled and whose floors were polished, and whose strange smell haunted me.

But I came to love the sisters into whose care I was passed. One may love animated forms without knowing their purpose. With their sail-like shoulder and headdress, the sisters gleamed like daisy petals. Their rubicund faces completed the statuary. They seemed to encompass the whole world in their arms, which they so fluidly spread, their tread subduing the earth to a harmless reach. I burgeoned in their strength and benevolence, but I hated my fellow orphans and had to be cajoled to sit with them at mealtime.

Soon I found myself in one of the high beds of the high ceilinged hospital to have my tonsils out.

Although I quailed at the imminence of my turn to go into the curtained off chamber where the unimaginable horrors the doctor was perpetrating occurred all that day, a newly experienced surge of independence seemed to grip me, for the nurses treated me with respect and kindness. They treated me like a person, not a child. All the same, they were having their diabolical way with me. Tonsils and circumcision were routine in orphanages and eventually, quaking with fear, I had to open my mouth wide to permit the white ogre's mutilation of my throat.

I felt more at home in the clean, formal surroundings of the hospital. I began folding my clothes and tidying my bed, proudly telling the nurses that my mother had taught me how to do this. I wanted to contribute to the peace and orderliness that reigned in this newly revealed medical world. The doors and walls of the makeshift hospital were full of enormous windows of big panes of glass and through the high ones the sky was leaden and snow was falling. It was freezing cold. I was visited here, lying in my high hospital bed, by my future stepmother and her two daughters. They were very grandly dressed but I was too shy to say a word.

The desert of the London railway station, where, with a group of children I stand lost, waiting to be taken away. White panes of glass form the roof of the immense vault. Towards them, billowing clouds of soft white steam unroll above a gigantic green and gold engine. Hollow sounds, clangour of metal, resound in all the distant corners of the vast station. I see strange people sitting behind the windows of a train. They are all beautifully and warmly dressed. They are happy, unworried, clean faced people, excited and illumined with intelligible purpose. I feel swallowed in the crowd and search for the invisible one who will rescue me. All my little companions on the train seem to have disappeared. That I alone am left feeds my consciousness of difference, my delusion of superiority.

We left the north, our home, without any farewells. Through the misty windows the platform was empty in the cold grey morning. Throughout the uncomfortable journey, the train drilled in the truth that it was taking me further from home. Abandoning, with distance and time, any hope of returning, tears flowed unbidden. A kind gentleman attempted to brighten me up with wise words and sweets, but my tears would not stop. I sat enclosed in inconsolable sorrow.

1

London

Behind my guardian I ran, through the drab streets of London. A low neat house behind an iron fence was the home of my new foster mother. I was impressed by the brass doorstep and solid door, and felt proud of my adventures. I had got over my crying and was determined to be brave. The woman of the house was a long time coming to the door, which eventually opened slowly, showing a small kindly face. She admitted us immediately and put me into her front bedroom, which contained an enormous bed under the window, then she shut the door and locked it. I stood there a long time, looking at the low bed and the long curtains. I could not see through the lace curtains. I stood stock still, afraid to make a sound, very uncomfortable, for I wished to relieve my bowels, but no adult seemed to have an inkling of this, as though it were an unexpected, shameful thing. Indeed, I was ashamed of my need. I looked under the bed for a chamber like the big china pot of Mother's, but saw nothing. I approached the door, but was too shy to knock. There was a sewing machine like Mother's against the wall with carved drawers in it and I relieved myself in one these very carefully, filling it neatly and putting it back into position. I was terrified of being discovered. I can recall no consequences of this.

I had a little room with a sloping roof at the top of a steep narrow flight of stairs in my foster mother's house. She showed me how to say my prayers, kneeling in warm pyjamas beside the immaculate bed. Light blue flowers spread over the walls, and a bright light illuminated the room. I said the lord's prayer after her as she sat on the bed beside me. Then she made me remember my people one by one, aunts, uncles, Mother and Father, and ask god to bless each one. This reawakened my grief at losing Mother and after I was affectionately tucked up in bed I gave vent to my sorrow in endless sobbing. Torturing uncertainties filled me, staring in the shadowy glow of the night light at the sloping ceiling.

I used to wander on a big treeless common near the house. A group of boys played football there. I longed to play with them but they were so absorbed in their game they were unaware of my existence. I swallowed what I saw as their rejection as something bitter.

The hot potato man wound his tricycle over the faint rough path of the common, and for a ha'penny he would stop and hand me down a hot dry-skinned, fragrant potato. I was using pocket money I had brought from home, which was so much more than I usually possessed that I felt the vanity of wealth. Off the common was a new street of rising houses. I had never seen houses being built before and while gazing into one of these I was spoken to kindly by a young man and woman, whom I immediately loved as a newly sent mother and father. They were about to go into one of the new houses and with the generosity of youth, had offered to take me with them. When I told my foster mother about these kind people she forbade me to go out. After that I did not get further than the iron gate of the small front garden, although I continued dreaming of being rescued by my new friends.

Packed buses from London passed by our house, pulling up at the corner. I stood on the footpath and stared at the faces through the windows of the bus, hoping to discover Mother. Well-dressed men and women would alight and walk quickly away as though unaware of my presence. I followed them with my eyes for a sign of recognition.

I saw my mother in every woman's face. My small foster mother would stand in the long warm fragrant kitchen, rolling out dough with floury arms. She would bend over the large black ovens and sweep out trays of tarts whose smell reminded me of the past. She did not mind my taking what I liked, so I climbed the shelves of the larder to find mince pies, my favourite with Mother. I became very fond of the short broad figure of my foster mother, her heavy draperies and ambling gait. She seemed fond of me too and used to talk to me in a rational humane way.

I was taken away from her for adoption in an underhand way. My foster mother and another woman took me for a walk. We were going shopping. At the underground station with its infernal flight of steps, the other woman took my hand and pulled me onto the steps. I would not let go of my foster mother's hand and while this tug of war went on, I screamed with all my might. Superior force broke my grip on the woman I loved and I was pulled slowly down to the waiting train.

I was taken by train to the home for orphans where there was already a group of other children. We had all travelled a long way from our birthplace. I suppose we were all wrapped in grief. As soon as we climbed the high wide steps and passed through the great doors of the old mansion, we were unceremoniously commandeered by large flamboyant women in white who undressed us, scrubbed us in iron tubs of steaming water, and put us to bed like so many manikins, laughing and gossiping the while. Completely naked but warm with impatient towel rubbing, I was asked by a red-faced woman if I had been to the lavatory that day. I was so embarrassed I could not answer her coherently, whereupon, just as I was, she turned me over and inserted some soap in my anus. I was affronted by the way she tossed me about, and annihilated by shame.

This home where my new parents came one fine Sunday morning to pick me up was full of little children like myself, all loitering bemused and lost in the enormous dining room where we were given breakfast, the sun pouring in through high windows. We were all gaily dressed, very shy and charming. I was not only shy, but also completely insulated within myself, from fear of my fellow orphans. The strange room with its sinister magnitude filled me with apprehension. I could not fight my loneliness. I wanted only my mother's absolute love, and I wanted no sharing of it.

I was about five when my new parents took me to live in a basement flat in London, near Marylebone station. It was 1925. My new stepfather was an ascetic looking man, tall and emaciated. He always dressed in black. My stepmother was large, opulent, and fond of bright luxurious dress. She admired my appearance, and fondled my curls. I was a little doll with pretty hair and blue eyes to her. They already had two adopted girls at home.

My new older sister was dark and remote, inspiring in me horror for this dark-faced gipsy, whose abrupt demonic movements carried dream-like threats. She remained ever alien to me like an evil spirit. Even as a little girl, she seemed grown-up and contemptuous of the world of toys and play, as well as of our father and mother.

The younger sister was very fair with straight blond hair and blue eyes, open faced and willing to play with me. But even she could not set me free from myself. We played together on the cold cramped kitchen floor, but she seemed to live in an inner world of her own and I had no curiosity about it. We each enjoyed ourselves in our own way. Our parents' treatment, at first very indulgent, later very harsh, enlarged the already established individualistic traits in each of our characters, and did nothing to prepare common ground between us on which we could communicate with each other.

Opposite our row of tenements was a long grey elementary school that I attended soon after my arrival. This school had a highly polished wooden floor on which I could not prevent myself slipping. It was a perennial threat to my physical existence. Outside the row of windows in the long school corridor was a walled-in playground, covered with asphalt, where I fell and skinned my knees. There was also a steep flight of high steps up to the school, which I found great difficulty in climbing without hurting myself or descending without falling. My awkwardness and clumsiness was manifest to everybody and to myself, and increased my feeling of estrangement from my fellow beings.

Yet I enjoyed taking my place in the ranks of strange little children on the polished floor and receiving so much attention from the elderly schoolmaster. Because Mother had taught me to read and write he soon put me up into the second class where a strict woman teacher quickly filled me with stupor, and I ceased to learn. After school I would timidly cross the foreign street with its hostile motor cars, and walk home slowly along the unfamiliar footpath beside the railings. I was always expecting to meet my real mother and stared into women's faces to find her resemblance. Her loss had cost me all my capacity for feeling and self-confidence. Many times I thought I recognised her, and hurried towards some astonished woman who would sweep by me like a leaf trying to regain the shore.

I had come from the country and the sea shore of the north of England and I hated the confined subterranean flat in which we lived. Millions of people in London were living in those little underground kennels, even giving themselves airs at possessing such a city home. A combined dining room and kitchen contained our three beds against its walls. There was a main bedroom in the depths of the flat, with a large bed and dressing table for our parents. Our mother used to lie in bed of a morning telling us what to do to get us off to school. Father was up before we were awake, preparing himself for the office, frying his own bacon and eggs. Mother would luxuriate in the feather bed under the eiderdown, her heavy head lolling on the long white bolster. The stale smell of dirty clothes hung in the air. Father attended to his appearance like an actor, adjusting his gold cufflinks like a cardinal, and bending over his tight fawn spats like a warrior. He went out to work in Oxford Street with great aplomb, carrying bowler hat and stick into the stone quarry outside. He walked to work like thousands of others in exactly the same attire and with exactly the same complacency.

Yolande, my younger sister, attended a nearby Sunday School and one day I was asked to go to her Sunday School party. I rebelled against the idea but Mother insisted as she thought it would help to break down my shyness, which she held in derision. She began at once devising how she could display me, her latest pretty possession, before all the good people who attended church. Mother paid excessive attention to clothes and made herself a most imposing figure in sumptuous furs, long black satin dresses, and lustrous pearls, although this was accomplished by encasing her body in crippling stays. Standing on her rumpled bed, behind her voluptuous red back, I had to hook them up for her. In girlish clothes and curled hair I was eventually prepared for the party. She curled her own hair and mine with a pair of hot tongs. She did not want to acknowledge the male in me, except as an opportunity to transform a potential enemy into the malleable feminine.

Very conscious of my specious attire, I was not the little prince my mother wanted her adopted son to be, but a displaced peasant. I was set down like an intruder among the pampered little boys and girls and was stubbornly unable to say a word to anyone. My sister disappeared. It was my first experience of agonising self-consciousness. I was an imposter, not because of language but because of dress and manners. My working-class honesty and roughness simmered beneath the pretty clothes and dumbness. At the long table laden with plates of cakes, two rows of merry boys and girls were tucking in, while I was too afraid to reach for a cake for fear of being observed. I greedily crammed a few cakes into my mouth when the still half-laden table was left, afflicting myself with guilt for my two-faced behaviour.

My father first began to hit me after I stole some

chocolate of my sister's. It was Christmas time and I felt unjustly treated because Yolande had received a bar of chocolate and I none. I sneaked among her presents when nobody was looking and took it. I had been used in my real home to taking whatever I wanted and I did not apprehend how serious the loss would be. Everyone was outraged. I was beaten on the bottom by Father's hand for this, desolated by shame and hatred as he exposed my posterior to everybody's sight. As far as I remember I had never been struck before.

I remember the immobilising force of my father's arms. I felt demoralised by the brute strength of another human being, who could take away my freedom whenever he wished, and treat me like an object, deaf to my struggling and crying. When my stepmother protested, my father assured her it would stop me doing it again. How could I ever do the same thing again?

I remember standing naked in the tin bathtub on the kitchen table. Hot water was heated in a big iron pot on the coal stove and poured into the tub. My stepmother asked me who had washed me before. Vague memories of Mother and me in an iron tub on the floor returned, and of Mother herself bathing, squeezing the golden, many eyed sponge against her white skin. The big figure of my stepmother terrified me. She lifted me up off the floor to her face to examine me, looking at my body with derisive inquisitive eyes, and paying particular attention to my genitals. I felt very small and embarrassed.

I decided to run away, to return to my real home and find my real mother. I walked out of the house and kept walking hurriedly down street after street, to put as much distance as possible between me and those hostile people. No one seemed to notice me and as the day wore on I surrendered to feelings of freedom and independence. Everyone was lost in their own thoughts, and I slipped through them. I was not interested in them either, or in their buildings.

Eventually, I found myself in a poorer quarter. I was walking alongside water, near which I had always lived. I was able to look into the living rooms of houses through their open front doors. I felt an altogether more friendly and accepting atmosphere. I felt I recognised the interior of one. The vaulted cover of a sewing machine was the same as the one over my mother's. I saw a plump woman sitting on a kitchen chair. She watched me with an amused expression. I ran to her, blurting out that I thought this was my home. She listened to me carefully, then took me on her knee, questioning me. I seemed to recognise the fireplace and mantelpiece in the room. The wallpaper seemed familiar. The woman spoke to other people in the house and they came and questioned me kindly and seriously about how I had got there. I told them where I had come from and why I had run away. They showed me other rooms of the house to convince me I had made a mistake and I began to realise I had been deceived. It was not long before a policeman appeared and I was marched away, my hand in his, to the police station. I could not object to anything such gentle people did to me. My step-parents soon arrived at the police station, where even they seemed to have become kinder, so I went home with them with a superficial happiness hiding an underlying turmoil.

Mother loved visiting the big shops, like Selfridges. Frightened of losing her in this foreign land, I desperately kept up. She pushed Yolande through the melee in a stroller. My elder sister was an attendant dark shadow, silent and scornful. My mother seemed to delight in showing us all the wealth of London as though it were her own: the operatic props of her fantastic, childish world. She would never buy anything that was good and expensive for us children, although she wore expensive things herself. She was particularly vain of her pearls, and of her black high-heeled shoes. She was very fond of being seen, and of dressing to be seen. She loved sumptuous furs, in which she would bury her heavy face. I suspect she was playing some Wagnerian role for herself, and saw herself not as the mother, but as the fairy godmother of her adopted children.

Mother identified herself with the aristocracy, and openly despised all other classes of people. She carried herself like a queen and was autocratic in manner. During afternoon walks in the park she would proudly point out to us the lords and ladies riding idly in Rotten Row. She took the astounding spectacle of the guards for granted: the glittering horse guards seen prancing through the finely wrought gates of the gardens, the plumes on their burnished helmets flowing, and their naked swords held rigidly before them on the pommels of their saddles, high above my eyes; or the grenadiers in their brilliant red uniforms and frowning busbies, marching python-like past the crowd, or standing like statues before the palace railings. For a long time the aristocracy and the guards were the zenith of human achievement to me. No one questioned the general infatuation with authority, or the admiration of the army, especially of the guards. Mother would feed the ducks on the lake, and sit in the sun watching the nursemaids of the rich wheeling perambulators in Hyde Park, while we made daisy chains on the mown grass. My sisters made them with embarrassing dexterity while I fumbled over mangled daisies. We played ball in an inhibited genteel way, every thoughtless urge oppressively damped.

Someone had died. A relative of Father's. He wanted to take me to see her and although my mother and sisters tried to persuade me not to go, I felt an eagerness, a devil may care readiness to face something vaguely grim that required courage, for, as Yolande warned me, I would have to look at a dead face. I informed them I had seen one before. The idea of accompanying my stepfather alone filled me with pride. I sat in the back of a shiny black sedan beside a tall sombre man in black. Out in the country we stopped beside a low cottage in a garden full of flowers. We went through a low gate and stood about bereft of purpose on the garden paths. They all seemed to be men, tall men like my father, in black suits. They spoke to one another in murmurs, and did not seem to notice me. The door of the low cottage was open wide. It was dark inside. Everyone seemed to enter hesitantly and I did not want to go in. At length, against my will, I was propelled through the gaping doorway by long ministering arms. My father seemed to have forgotten me. Others pushed me towards the dead woman lying in the window. Her face repelled me with horror. It was the ugliest, cruellest thing I had seen. I did not want to look at it but they held me there expecting me to cry. I could not. I felt I had disappointed them. They were eating and drinking. They made me drink something. Then we left.

At holiday times we used to go to the seaside south of London and stay in a big guest house with a garden and fountain. We three children were meticulously dressed and groomed by Mother. Father became much more benign. He doffed his black suit and bowler hat. At these times I forgot all about my real family and thought my stepfather and mother were my own and that Yolande and Brenda were my real sisters. I became fond of them all, especially my sisters, but it was impossible to please my mother. At the most she would be amused at my efforts to do so. We children developed a spontaneous camaraderie. At the same time, I succumbed to the generous attention of my father, while Mother and the girls seemed mutually bound.

Sometimes Father played in the sand with us. He liked making boats in the sand and would show me how to complete one in every detail, with endless patience. We were both very proud, sitting in our boat on the specially made seats. Mother and Father would pay for a couple of deck chairs and recline in them while we three children made sand castles. Mother would never get out of her chair. She basked in the sun and the salt air and the notice her voluptuous figure and opulent attire always evoked.

Once holidays were over, Father would again become remote, out of reach. Then, my sisters and I would play together on the grass of Kensington Gardens and Hyde Park while Mother sat heavily on one of the benches, perhaps remembering the last opera while she crocheted. Although she would never leave the girls, Mother sometimes left me to play in the sand pit in the gardens, where I became agonisingly aware of my fear of other boys. I think I coveted all their space and sand, while at the same time I could not forget my smallness and clumsiness, a lesson which Mother kept instilling.

The recurrent treat at Christmas was the pantomime for which Mother would dress us beautifully and then escort us to the theatre. I loved walking with her through the

London streets. She had such authority: London was her own personal stage. We three orphans, holding hands, would follow the swinging satin covered hips through the falling snow and early dusk to Selfridges. I was terrified of losing her in the crowd. Sometimes she would take us to a Lyons restaurant and treat us like celebrities.

Father seemed to be growing fonder of me. He would allow me to visit him in his office in Oxford Street, which I could walk to from home. He seemed to be an important man in the office. All the clerks, each sitting at his own little table, were delighted to see me and would take me to him in his own special glassed-off room. He liked me coming to see him by myself and I was beginning to gain confidence in finding my way through the populous London streets. Father wanted me to become an English gentleman like himself; he had been to one of the greater public schools. He was an unashamed imperialist and reinforced my passion for the overt pageantry of London. He could not help but make me a devoted subject of the king and a defender of the empire. I fell for the general conceit about everything English. After all, Londoners could purchase the best samples of everything made the world over, and the English workman probably did deliver the best quality in the world.

When Father and Mother were at the opera in the evening we three children would get up and play. Half awake, I would hear them returning, very happy with their evening and murmuring rapturously over this singer or that. I had begun to be happy in London but that was soon to change when we left the city for the suburbs. It was also the end of my mother's happiness.

2

Hounslow

When I was eight we left London for a suburb six miles away, Hounslow. We occupied one of the newly built row of houses in London Road. We now had a garden in front and behind, and opposite us was a tram depot. At this time we also acquired a car, for which a garage had been made ready in the back garden. Once in the suburbs, all our lives became more arid. We had much less time with each other because school, office, and shops were much further away than they had been. My father acquired some position of importance in his office and more and more became the obsequious functionary, incapable of understanding human needs, least of all those of children approaching puberty like ourselves, and those of a woman like our mother. In authority over several men at the office, he apparently felt all his own needs fulfilled. In his firm he was now the master he wanted to be, and he wanted to play that role at home too.

In the new house we had plenty of space. Upstairs were three bedrooms and a bathroom, and downstairs a dining room, living rooms and a kitchen. With the authority which he so much prized, Father tried to kill the awakening sexual life in his children. There was a small front bedroom looking on to the tram depot where I could conveniently be separated from my sisters, if necessary, by a locked door. Suspicion infected his mind even against the two girls, for Brenda was soon sent away to boarding school. Whatever Father did became a means of exerting authority over others. The garden he planted became a means of restricting his children's movements, instead of liberating them, as a garden should. The car, which realised so well his passion for power, became a prison to its other occupants.

I now went to a low red brick school, behind a garden, with a large asphalt playground lined by giant, fragrant trees. I used to walk to school with my sisters. Greedy for sweets, we would hurry to the little store on our way, where I would spend any money I had stolen from Mother's purse, which she left lying around, as though oblivious of what a little thief I was. I had an irresistible desire for sweets, especially chocolate. Children not permitted to love may easily become gluttons. I would consume my trophies clandestinely, under the desk or on my lonely walks, not offering a fragment to anyone.

Walking daily through empty streets, beside motionless cultivated gardens, under ranks of plane trees, life seemed dull and menacing after London, whose monotonous walls were always impregnated with mystery and freedom. Everything was pointless. Father had made a mistake in leaving London, especially as it affected Mother, who loved entertainment.

I could not understand the old ladies who were my teachers at the new school. They seemed intent on capturing and exploiting my emotions for the good of manhood and my country and its empire. I could not grasp the reality of these things. I was bent on doing my own thinking. My emotions were buried with the memories of my lost people. The teachers could only bring tears to my eyes with their incomprehension of me as a thinking being, who had different ideas of god from theirs.

I became conscious of the bully in myself at this school; how low men can be tempted to stoop. There was at the school a big fat boy who would never defend himself. He would stand with his back to the wall and let anyone punch him without any attempt to run away or retaliate. To me he was a new phenomenon for pugnacity was everywhere: had we not just defeated the Germans, whose bestial acts were gaudily depicted in every comic and boy's story book? But this soft, large, all too human form just stood there and took whatever a bully gave him. I had been the bully's prey too, but by deceit or flight I usually mitigated his aggression. I felt a desire to go up and give this boy a punch, but something stopped me, the very ugliness of the act, shame, or perhaps fear that his huge bulk might suddenly act and annihilate me. I decided then that the ugliest thing, the most unmanly thing, is to strike another human being. I had also learnt the lesson Mother drummed into me, that I was the weak one, the small one, the coward. I knew I was a greater weakling than the fat boy, and might inspire him with a slumbering heroism. Of course, he was the only hero among us.

It was in Hounslow that I began my long walks into the surrounding country. I would set off in one direction or another, always alone, and usually did not speak a word to a soul until I returned. I would walk towards London by two different routes, one through endless walls, the other through market gardens. On the first route, through walled streets, I had two special landmarks: the huge cylinders of the gas works and the wonderfully high wall of the Pears soap factory.

The gas works captured me with the symmetry of its vast structures, and the space of its constellation. I was proud to have walked so far and to have braved the smell, which everybody seemed to avoid. I approached the gas works in spite of its sinister associations, as though the monuments taught me a lesson I was seeking. By contrast, the soap factory seemed to conceal the secrets of grace and love behind its high grey wall that was decorated with the lovely and loving woman who used Pears soap. I was also fond of the Hounslow railway station, beneath whose ponderous bridge I would stride. With a thrill of dread I heard the trains thundering hollowly overhead. I liked the worn cobblestones of the road below the railway bridge, with their age and patient suffering. On weekends, when there was little traffic, I would shuffle my shoes over these rounded stones, delighted by their different forms and their difference from the miles of smooth smelly tar, with which they were soon replaced.

When I began to approach the city I would turn back, as I found the maze of streets and traffic bewildering and threatening. I used simply to enjoy the motion of walking over the hard paving stones, beside the high walls, as though I were moving alone in the world, on my own path, like a star on its course, and the peace of being away from a home so often filled with furious storms.

Perhaps I enjoyed most this first route because I was

unobserved. On the second road the country was open, and I could easily be seen by people in passing cars on the wide new highway, or working in their gardens. The highway was terrifying with its absence of hiding places. I felt like an intruder. I had only to suspect I was being watched to become painfully self-conscious.

Father had infused me thoroughly with guilt, for he had begun beating me again on the completely false conviction that I was masturbating, or playing with myself as he and Mother called it. Mother was excessively possessed by this notion, and obliged Father to beat me whenever she was taken by her obsession. She also began using a cane on me. I had no idea what it was they were accusing me of.

The passion to take whatever I wanted revived; I stole money at home and food from shops that displayed cakes in their doorways. There were many temptations along this road to the city, dotted with market gardens. Particularly desirable were the large, ripe gooseberries, and bunches of black and red currants. It was not difficult to pick and gorge oneself on these fruits, although I was always fearful of detection. Once I saw some thick sticks of deep red rhubarb, and foreseeing a reward in precious affection at home from Mother, trembling, I gathered a bundle, and in trepidation carried it home and proffered it to her. I persisted in loving this woman who hated and tortured me.

I was very fond of trees, and my favourite street was a short one on my country route. On both sides were aged plane trees, whose fragrant breath hung in the shaded avenue like a protective mist. The large, sodden, hand-shaped leaves were all over the footpath and road, making one's steps silent. At the end of this avenue was an unattended market garden, where among the tangle of weeds were old gooseberry bushes bearing plum-sized gooseberries. There I always hoped to see a tall elegant old lady who had once spoken to me on the footpath, inquiring about my family. She had bowed gently, and smiled kindly at me, making me feel important. I felt she had discovered and accepted my existence, something no one else knew how to do. Any curiosity on the part of anyone about my family filled me with the hope I might be found and returned home to my real mother. On several visits to this avenue I tried to determine which was her house, for I hoped she would take me to her and love me, as I loved her. But when at last I saw her working in her garden, I was too shy to approach.

My parents were fond of nature; my mother for sensuous reasons, my father because he could cut and train plants like roses, raspberries and apple trees. They were always happy to discover wild flowers in the country, in the forests and fields where Father would drive us in his new car at weekends. If it was fine the canvas hood would be thrown back; if wet, the celluloid windows put in. I too loved to discover flowers on my walks for I was always looking for something to please or placate Mother. I loved the beauty and scent of the blooms in the hedgerows and damp lanes. Coming upon clumps of wild flowers in London was like a scientific discovery. Finding a group of rhododendrons with their opulent red blooms on the plain of Hounslow Heath, I went away elated, as though I was carrying them with me. I did not take any of these huge blooms, but finding some blue bells on another occasion, hiding like shy children under the ancient oaks of a wood, I carried a bunch of them home like priceless booty, in love with the pure, intense blue, exalted by their fragrance, and mystified by their long, succulent stalks. I suppose we were all looking for a way out of the claws of London; a way back to the simplicity of life with virgin earth. But London's claws were growing longer and sharper, and in a year or two she would relentlessly begin to close them in the Depression.

Another of my walks led away from London, along London Road to Hounslow Heath, past shops crowded with women, prams, and little children. I was always hungry, and it was never possible to pass the cake shops without a long wistful contemplation of their windows. If I had taken some silver from Mother's purse the night before, I would buy buns or rock cakes. If I had no money I would ask for stale cakes, which were given away.

On the heath I looked for heather, a flower I associated with half-remembered places in the north. The gleaming, golden flowers of gorse also symbolised some remote, mystical beauty. Flowers were my friends and teachers; I loved them. Here on Hounslow Heath I discovered the ruined hide-out of the notorious highwayman Dick Turpin. The crude, gigantic rocks of the fallen refuge lay scattered like a derelict fortress. His ghost stood watching me as I ventured with trepidation into the ruins. He had been wanted by the police, an outcast. I could have befriended him. He would have allowed someone so small and cowardly, so weak and clumsy as me, to love him, because the rest of the world hated and hunted him.

The new house with its mahogany furniture was a yoke around our necks. Mother's and Father's material circumstances had certainly changed. A large gramophone cabinet, also of mahogany, the sign of affluence and taste, was standing in the dining room, with records of grand opera stored in its little cupboard. I was eventually expected to sing arias for Mother and Father, usually in the morning while they were still in bed, after I had taken them their cup of tea. I would stand at the bottom of the stairs doing my best to please them, for I also liked the tunes, but often I came face to face with my own inability to remember them, and crushing mortification. They wanted me to sing louder, so I strained my voice up the stairs to the utmost. Then my memory would fail, and I would be unable to complete the song. This irritated my parents, and was an additional proof of my ineptness. My slowness of physical growth and mental development was a great frustration to them. They were discovering that they were not going to be justly rewarded for the pain and expense of adopting me. I was remaining the slow, awkward, self-conscious anarchist I had been born. There was no sign of my adopting either the royalist or the bureaucratic middle-class values that held unquestioned sway over their immured lives. Between them, these values made for an uneasy coexistence, which as time went on, more and more often exploded their contradictions. Violent rows filled the house, quelling our innocent expectation of love. Mother wanted to treat me like a doll: to beat me one minute, and curl my hair the next, without any apprehension of my feelings. Father wanted to recruit me into his all male world.

They compensated themselves for their disappointment over me with their celebration of Yolande. They compared our heights, regularly setting us against the wall beside the white mantelpiece in the ostentatious living room, a pencil line drawn along a ruler on top of our heads. Yolande leapt ahead of me, although she was a year younger. They could not accept me as I was. They had wanted an aristocrat for a son, not a dwarf who could barely understand a thing at school. Yolande was taller and more intelligent. She had more intelligence in her little finger than I in my entire being.

I was envious of her for her intelligence and personality, which were always working together for generous motives and were irresistible to everybody. I was jealous of the precedence she and my elder sister received in our parents' affection and attention. I was envious of my elder sister for her independence, which made her a fearless wild animal not afraid to bite anyone, however big, who opposed her. From the start I felt repressed by my inferior class. I was a working-class son in an ambitious, pretentious middle-class home. I was afraid for my skin, for my working-class identity with which I had been imbued by my real mother. I became self protective and possessive, envious of the possessions of others and afraid of others harming me for my covetous thoughts. I felt the whole family were my enemies.

As time passed, our parents went out more and more often at night, to their whist drives and parties and even to London, leaving us children alone. Our first mission on their departure was the large larder under the stairs. Here we would rifle the top shelf containing the precious things reserved for our parents. After satisfying our palates if not our appetites, we would chase one another through the house with pillows, slide down the banisters. I would search for money that had been left lying about. At the sound of the key in the door we would all scurry to bed. Occasionally, through an unexpectedly early return, we were caught raiding the larder, or skylarking, and were locked in our bedrooms and beaten the next day by Father with the sole of his leather slipper. Although I hated the prospect of physical pain, and the vice-like grip he confined me in, I secured a secret pleasure from the intimacy involved with my father that these beatings entailed. It was the only time he embraced me. I was so chronically enslaved to the need for affection that I easily forgot pain for the pleasure of human physical contact that had been denied. My mother rarely touched me affectionately and when one day, returning from a holiday, she brought me a present of a whip, I felt almost cut in two. 'This will be good to whip you with,' she said.

Although we were taken regularly to the seaside when we were young, once we reached the age of nine or ten, our parents began to leave us with other families whom they paid to look after us while they went on holiday. I remember being so miserable at having to return to my parents that I would break down in tears when the awful day arrived, although I was never bold enough to complain to anyone about them, or to confess that I did not want to go home. It was particularly hard to leave those households in the country where I was sometimes boarded out. I became attached to the fields and animals, and to the country people who seemed at one with everything natural and fruitful. They could never have understood how one could not be happy to go home. On one occasion I was boarded with a family close by where there was a baby boy just beginning to toddle about. He became my playmate and I became so fond of him that on returning home I could not stop longing to see him. Eventually, I found my way back to the lane behind his house, and I used to stand gazing at him through the palings. He was the loveliest thing I had ever seen. I was soon forced to reveal to my father where I had gone and my parents seemed inordinately worried about it.

On our long drives into the country we picnicked in the woods, or on the grass beside the Thames where the white swans would glide by and nonchalantly snatch bread from their patrons. I could not really enjoy these outings, for my parents were always critically observing me, derisive of my awkwardness and silence, my small stature and self-consciousness. While they appraised me according to their middle-class values I only became more awkward. Above all, I think they were suspicious of me, of my intentions, my fate, as if I was likely to bring destruction to them.

On the river my father fished as though only an adult could fish, and only a man at that, while my occupation was to keep quiet and still, so the fish would come to his line. I stood for hours thus, staring blankly at the huddled grey walls of Windsor castle on the grass of the bank opposite. I never knew my father to catch a fish. Perhaps it was more important to him to fish in the correct manner, to see his float was upright and correctly submerged. Mother would sit on a blanket on the grass, telling us children what to do.

I began consciously to develop values contrary to those of my parents, although I continued to aspire to theirs in order to retain some of their attention, if not affection. I usually beat both my sisters in races, so I considered myself a good runner. I could climb trees better than some boys, and could travel on foot over distances that some people were carried over, so I began to value bodily motion through space and distance. Explorers became my heroes, because by their own efforts they travelled so far into different worlds. They walked everywhere, and went far. They discovered new things. While my parents imposed their sedentary values upon me, wishing me to exist as something to be seen and admired for its appearance, I was developing dreams of movement and escape. I wanted to find my wealth as an explorer picking up bars of gold left by some ancient race, rather than earn it by my presence sitting imposingly in a chair. I could not be imposing. I could only be will-o'-the-wisp. I was painfully embarrassed playing their false role.

Long lines of cars returning slowly from Brighton to London through the twilight of a warm summer evening remain in my memory, with remnants of intense feelings of self-oppression brought on by my inarticulate affection and love for the fragrant and pulsating world passing by. I could not open my mouth to utter a word of this feeling in all the two or three hour drive. I feared my words would meet only condemning silence. I would not have said the right thing. I hated myself for my inability to speak, for none of the correct things ever occurred to me. I seemed unable to learn them.

When Father was behind the wheel he forgot everything except the destination. The natural needs of his children to relieve themselves were overlooked while he drove on for hours. Nothing could interfere with his precise plan of getting to the goal, and the car became the torture chamber of a prison for its other occupants.

The flashing lights of London were supposed to capture everyone's imagination, but they disappointed me. I liked the streets with the crowds of people rather than the incomprehensible neon writing on the roof tops, where sentences were never completed, and the lights flickered arbitrarily off and on. To me the coloured spectres danced ominously above our heads as though they could see and exulted in some dark fate for man.

The whole meaninglessness of our life repelled me. After tea the compulsory games would begin. The most hated was whist, which, like an intelligence test, did everything to frighten intelligence away. For my parents it was the touchstone of intelligence, and confirmed their suspicions that I had none, for they knew nothing of degrees or varieties. One was either bright or stupid.

The next most hateful game was ludo. Here they could hardly invoke intelligence, so the humiliation was less painful, but I had to pretend to enjoy these games, and thus began my two-faced existence. A child can passionately hate a parent who beats him, yet, in order to avoid destruction, he has to pretend to love him, to like playing with him and enjoy obeying him.

When I was ten I went to a boys' high school where I used to walk every day with my newly acquired satchel. Much to my parents' surprise, I had won a scholarship from the primary school. I was very surprised too. I did not equate it with 'intelligence' however: that was something to do with winning at cards. Getting a scholarship did not change Mother or Father's opinion of me.

I was terrified of all the teachers and the boys at the high school. Most of the teachers were big men made even bigger by their voluminous gowns. Most terrifying was the headmaster who sat alone in a big room in the centre of the school. He took us for English but he seemed most concerned to make us love god and the commandments. He had a concern for our inner life that made me uncomfortable. I was very conscious of my smallness, and saw myself as an easy victim. I imagined all the athletic-looking masters perpetrating violence upon me, I suppose of the kind my father exercised. I knew it need only to be at their whim for me to be locked in the inescapable bars of their arms, to receive what punishment they pleased for wrongdoings I might be guilty of only in their imaginations. Guilt, like my appearance or stature, was part of my existence that could only be described by others. If a teacher punished me, it would be because he saw me as culpable, although I might know nothing of the reason.

The French teacher had an enormous face which seemed always about to explode, big hands which seemed to encompass everything that would elude me, and a diabolical voice that annihilated me. He strode like a giant over the classroom, the most colourful of masters, and he made me feel ashamed for not learning from him. He danced French, wrestled French, shouted and sang French, carrying the real boys, those worthy of being Frenchmen, along with him. I sat shrinking while the fire, razing ignorance, passed over me. He wrapped himself in his black gown like an avenging angel and never relaxed his vigilance. Yet this teacher probably threatened me less than any of them. His vision was impersonal, and the whole brute force of his body was in the grip of an impersonal demon.

There was only one classroom teacher I could bear. My form master would quietly read to us when he was not teaching us maths. He would stand in an engagingly graceful way against the tall window, reading from the book as though it were a revelation, with a sort of perfection of language I had never before heard. He was very young, small and slight, with a beautiful smile and rosy complexion. I loved him but was also afraid of him.

His eye was on me personally, too. Each one of us was a different and interesting individual to him. He seemed to radiate goodness. He would keep the whole form spellbound during his reading and even in his maths lessons. These were the only lessons in which I felt I was earning credit in the adult heaven, the quietness he cultivated enabling me to understand and complete what I was doing.

In the physics class, where it was a race to produce a thermometer or weigh a cube, I could accomplish nothing. All materials were refractory in my hands. The burly physics teacher was an ogre who performed juggling tricks for us to repeat, treating with scorn those who could not follow how he had done them. I was demoralised by envy of those boys who could repeat them. They were usually the bigger and better dressed boys.

I found some avenue of compensation for my smallness and failure in the gymnasium. My lightness enabled me to climb the ropes and parallel bars more easily than many of the bigger boys. I even attempted vaulting. The gym teacher was a slight young man with a kind smile who wanted to develop my weedy frame and nursed me like an ailing plant. But I threw up a wall of coldness between us, perhaps because I could not tell him the terror inside me, which I had brought from home. So slavish had the corporal punishment and contempt I experienced at home made me, that I tried to please only those who inspired fear in me, while those from whom I felt no threat and who tried to approach me with love, I ignored. Parents and teachers who use violence can thus totally subvert human nature. One uses appearances to seem to love those one hates, and one does not allow love to show its face. My gym master encouraged me to box, and one evening my parents came with many others to smile complacently at their sons behind the ropes, battling like fighting cocks. I was terrified of boxing and had no notion of what I was doing, aware only of the ring of faces watching me. Elated at winning one bout, I lost the next and immediately lost all combative spirit.

The relative freedom of movement on the broad floor of the gym, the freedom of mind in the unknown space of the lofty room and the physical challenges they contained, were a liberation from the expanding load of intellectual problems under which I was inexorably sinking. I was encouraged by the gym teacher to excel in one of the gymnastics, but there was too much misery in my heart for me to concentrate on any of them. My misery sprang from the continuous yet unpredictable see-saw of rejection and acceptance at home.

At night my hands were tied behind my back to stop me masturbating, although I had no inkling of the meaning of the word. They were untied, swollen and numb in the morning, at my parents' bed. Whenever my mother felt inclined she would thrash me with a cane for this same imagined misbehaviour. At the same time, I had to play cards and other games with them of an evening as though there were no ill feeling between us. My father did not know the extremes my mother went to in his absence. This irrational dissonant treatment, where I was expected to be grateful for being thrashed and the target of contempt, made me a nervous wreck, always on the verge of tears.

I had no conviction of my own existence. I was convinced only of the existence of what came to me from outside.

The strong personality of the car emphasised that I was only a negative force, existing only by virtue of positive forces like itself. I was wholly subdued and under the spell of material values, like the seductive leather of the car's seats, the transparency of its high wide windscreen, and the paint of its bonnet. It seemed we did not take the car but the car took us — to the woods, the beach, or river. In the same way, the house with its contents was moulding us into its shape. This inversion of values where life retreats before the monster of materials, describes our life. I did not — and I doubt my parents did either — develop any values that were my own.

3

Life of a Bourgeois Child

My parents were bedevilled by the fear of the effect masturbation would have on me. They attributed my small stature and poor performance at school to it. This fear nourished their suspicion that my solitary habits and walks were only a resource or device for pursuing this indulgence. They sought deterrents, my mother sometimes with a frenzy imbued with abhorrence of my depravity. Apparently, by secret signs on my person, such as a shadow beneath the eyes, or the appearance of my genitals, they knew to their satisfaction whether I was guilty of playing with myself, as they called it, or not. They inspected my genitals regularly, after my returning from walks, or even after my lonely excursions in the woods when we were picnicking, and on school days before going to bed, for they became anxious about what could occur in the school lavatory in the company of other boys. What they were referring to and what they were looking for remained a complete mystery to me. They punished me on the basis of their suspicions, and as I lowered my pants or my pyjamas to let them inspect me, my identity floundered in a sea of shame and self-annihilation. I was no longer me, but a body, a thing appraised and judged as worthy of purchase or not. Should I be found guilty after one of those inspections, I would be beaten by my father with his slipper, and if it was a weekend or a holiday, locked in my room with only bread and water brought me for meals. Afraid that I might escape from my room through the window, they locked me in the bathroom. A board was put over the bath to act as a bed so that I could be locked there all day and night. I was sometimes there for several days at a time. Here I acquired the habit of abstract thought, and a thorough incompetence in practical life. I got to love the taste of bread and water. On one occasion my mother rushed into the bathroom in a frenzy, wielding her large scissors and asserting hysterically that she was going to cut off my penis. I had to promise never to do it again before she relented and went away, locking the door after her. On another occasion the family doctor came to the house. He sought me to understand that he would have to operate on me if I did not stop playing with myself. I did not know what he meant but I was too attuned to causeless guilt to tell him so. His awesome presence and the accusing eyes of my parents made me accept all their ineffable knowledge without a word. His words threw me into bewilderment and horror, for I knew not what to do to avoid his mutilation. I can see him sitting there now, filling the luxurious chair of the finely furnished sitting room, talking to me seriously, confidingly, blindly assuming I understood. He smiled urbanely at my desperate, superstitious parents as though he had just removed, once and for all, all their fears, then took his huge body flamboyantly out of the door and into the porch, where, with a few murmurs, he left.

After my two sisters went to boarding school, my mother's attacks on me became more vicious. When Father was at work I never knew when the whim would take her to give me a thrashing, swinging the cane wildly this way and that. It usually began with her demanding a confession that I had been playing with myself. When this was not forthcoming she demanded to inspect my genitals, which she handled and examined, while I, with suppressed tears, hoped she would not find the unknown signs she expected. If she did, her fury would begin. Having got the cane, she would strip me and soon I would be writhing about on her unmade double bed. Once she held my feet one after the other and caned the soles. This would go on until I confessed. At a lovely picnic spot on the Thames where we rented a caravan for a weekend, when Father had gone fishing, she became possessed with her delusion, ordering me to get a branch from the willow trees which overhung the river, and to undress. She began beating me wildly so that all the morning beauty of the place with which I had been enthralled, collapsed. Father returned and although he must have guessed the cause of my miserable face, did not remonstrate with her. I could feel he was also unhappy, for Mother would not go out because of her habitual headache.

My walks, and our drives into the country, were therefore always clouded with menace. I was afraid to take a step out of place or open my mouth. Every enjoyment had a reverse side that I could not forget. Can a man going to the gallows enjoy his ride there? And yet, I suppose we are all in that position. We are all riding to our death, yet somehow we contrive to enjoy ourselves. So, perhaps, did

I. I loved trees. I was intrigued by the shapes of their leaves and seeds. The acorn, the winged sycamore seed, the crab apple, were extraordinary and miraculous contrivances to me. In the hedgerows the wild rose, the glossy blackberry and the precious bay were great discoveries. It was a feat to raid the rare walnut without getting the indelible stain on one's hands, and to find bigger and bigger horse chestnuts with which to play conkers.

A blind old gentleman sat in a comfortable chair between the table and the fireplace. He was in a dark suit and the pale skin of his face was stretched with anguish. I had never seen such an erudite face. His large eyelids were closed. I felt he knew too much about me, knew I was double-faced. I approached him, as he asked me to do, apprehensively, and he felt me all over with long very white fingers that explored the features of my face. I was terrified lest he should discover my real self, the self that cringed from the world, beneath my new suit and well-practised disguises. His beautiful voice held irritation and reproach and made me search within myself for the transgression it implied. Perhaps everyone was guilty before him, his innocence and suffering. Large open books of Braille lay on the table. His sightless eyes looked at me with uncanny understanding. It was as though he saw everything. The room was warm with a fire and the smell of coal pervaded it. So I was introduced to the blind gentleman to whom I was later sent by my parents for a reason that was never explained to me. I was simply taken into London one day and put on the train for two weeks in Ross-on-Wye where he lived.

He was looked after by a stout middle-aged lady who met me at the station and walked home with me through the strangely quiet and fragrant country roads, by cottages with gardens crowded with flowers. I had never seen such tall dark trees; they rose like pinnacles into the sky. I was surrounded by quietness, stillness and peace, and I felt human love and tenderness everywhere. I had at this time had some lessons on the piano at home, but I was unable to remember the scales, and music was still a foreign language to me. The blind man asked me to play him some scales on the piano in his room, which I did not do very well. He then struck a tuning fork and asked me to sing the note, repeating this several times. I did not seem to be able to get the notes. I felt he was disappointed.

It was obvious that this carefully tended, regimented intellectual life and my wandering habits and unhappy mind were not in harmony. I felt the blind gentleman soon lost interest in me and I was taken for walks by the housekeeper in the fields beside the Wye. We walked along the margin of the river, my hand in hers. The Wye was remarkably narrow. I was surprised to find how rapidly it flowed. I did not think a river should be so narrow, and it disturbed me in its resemblance to a moat, for its banks were perfectly cut and steep as though they had been built by man. The housekeeper seemed constantly afraid that I would fall in and she would lose me. She sincerely cared for me, and used to give me my meals in the spotless, light-filled kitchen, but I could not respond to her affection.

Why are we unable to rejoice together in the beauty of the world? A boy feels his heart opening with love for others, possessed by a common passion for beauty, but his tongue is tied, his voice is stifled by didactic authority, or egoistic tyranny. Nothing but brute force has established this tyranny over the child, as it has over their mothers. Psychically, children and adults are equal, but the tremendous advantage in physical strength of the adult has enabled him to deny equality to the child. The child has no redress, and must attempt to mimic the psyche of those adults who surround him — parents, teachers and priests — in order to survive their physical threat. Ross-on-Wye revealed to me in the beauty of the English village and the love of English village people, the unfathomable barrenness of my city heart. But for all that I could not relinquish it. In this village I felt beauty everywhere — in the majestic trees, in the flowers, and in the people — but I could not surrender myself to it, there was too much hatred in my heart.

I returned to London amused at what the adults were doing to me, imagining they could alter me by changing my circumstances. I was proud of myself for having returned all the way to London by bus, and delighted in telling this to Yolande, for we had become much closer now. During her holidays from boarding school we began to have some serious discussions about god and the church. She was becoming more orthodox, while I was already a sceptic. I could not imagine god or the holy ghost but Yolande could describe each of them clearly. She did not seem to support my love of Christ. Yolande and I would lie in bed together arguing about our beliefs. She was the first person I was able to talk to; she had a generous personality. When Yolande was on holiday we were much together, and occasionally she would come with me on one of my walks.

One of my favourite walks was along St John's Road, which travelled in a straight line down towards the old districts of Isleworth near the Thames. Here the streets were narrow and winding, quiet and fragrant. Old mansions in sombre, park-like gardens lay behind high walls and closed wrought iron gates. Huge trees spread over the leaf-strewn lawns. No one ever stirred in these enchanted places. My temptation to enter them, which never left me, was never strong enough to overcome the taboo placed on them by the rich, or to challenge the broken glass or the points of the iron palings. They were the sacred places of a superior tribe.

It was on such a walk that I went one day into a Catholic church, devoured by curiosity. No one demurred and, sitting boldly in a pew, the sole member of the congregation, I was entranced by miraculous singing behind me. I turned to see the procession coming down the aisle.

The boys were singing in Latin, and a white clad priest crossed the front of the church swinging a smoking lantern. I inhaled incense for the first time. Ranks of candles were flickering. Strange compassionate figures looked down on me. The singing went on, so beautifully high. I sat listening in the empty, decorated cave, unable to leave, although fearful of being seen and put out. No one took any notice of me. After that, I returned there many times and feelings of devotion and dedication began to grip me, so that at length I asked Mother if I could go to church. She was unable to understand that I only wanted to go to this church, and sent me to Sunday School, which I quickly tired of.

Further down St John's Road was the cavernous brewery. The ringing harness of the horses heralded their coming to the castle-like gate, through which they would trot like richly decorated kings. Six mighty draught horses with shaggy hooves would pass by, making me feel my life as no human being could do, their brown skins stretched tight over their bursting bodies, their clear dark eyes flashing intelligence into mine. Yes, they seemed to say, we know one another. We are the same. They were like an unconscious primitive work of art, affirming my identity, and the reality of the world.

Past the high wall of the brewery I would walk on towards old Isleworth where there was a children's playground. I spent many hours here because I enjoyed the company of small children. I felt at home among their natural behaviour.

School was now becoming very oppressive to me. The only thing I could progress in at all was maths. This was not sufficient to prevent me coming second last in my form. I was called to the headmaster and, possessed by fear, heard him remonstrating with me unintelligibly until I was released. The certainty of rejection, imminent for some time, began to crystallise. I was no longer wanted there.

I went with my parents to the Christmas performance of *The Mikado*, put on by the senior students, and felt the poignancy of the farewell, for in spite of my failure, I had become fond of the walls and people of this old school. I went away full of admiration for the senior boys who could create the miracle I had seen on the stage and the music that accompanied it. Gripped by its enchantment, I was filled with an ardent love for everyone around me in the long hall.

The life of the bourgeois child is the life of acquiring psychological wealth, kudos, either in line with his parents and teachers or in contradiction to them. He incorporates what occurs, giving each event a value according to the relation in which he stands with the adults about him, whose evaluation of the event is a criterion. He does not analyse what occurs. He becomes a collector of labels, of names and titles. It is a case of what events he has seen, rather than the nature, cause and consequence of those events. To say one went to Richmond Park was to raise oneself in value with everyone's consent. The fact that one was very bored there, or terrified of one's parents there, is tucked away to be forgotten. Similarly, to say one went to a county high school, as my father used to proclaim of Worcester College, results in a self-appreciation acceptable to all, whether or not the school was able to teach you a solitary thing. City life is full of these badges of self-inflation that city people pin on themselves to everybody's satisfaction. We cannot enjoy any man-made thing without risking disillusionment by virtue of the greed and vanity behind it, whereas pleasure in nature is free from such risk.

After the humiliating disgrace of being rejected by the county high school, which should have provided me with a good education, I continued my long solitary walks in all directions from home. Mother went into hospital with an abdominal complaint, then a nursing home where she seemed to remain for a long time. I was very much happier, being left to myself all day, reading and talking to Yolande when she was on holiday from boarding school.

There were rumours about Australia. Eventually Father took me with him to London on the bus, which he caught every morning. I was smartly dressed. He took me to his office which was the same as I remembered it from years before, and from there to Australia House, where he left me in a small office with a gentleman who spoke to me about adventures in Australia, and asked me to think about whether I should like to go there. I was to come back another day and let him know. He gave me a book to read by Kingsley Fairbridge about his own adventurous childhood and youth in Rhodesia, which I took home and enjoyed reading during the weeks I was waiting for my fate to be decided. My feelings were very divided over the prospect of going so far away. I was getting to know and love the countryside around London. I was fond of Yolande and could not bring myself to tell her I might be going away. I hated to admit I was so much a victim of unknown forces that could take me away without sense or purpose. Nevertheless I could not help yielding to the excitement and curiosity of travelling and seeing an unknown land. When I saw the gentleman in Australia House again I agreed to go to Australia. There were no farewells. As I sat on the bus on my way to London, Yolande was playing on the footpath. I dared not wave to her lest she see my vanquished state. She was then eleven and I twelve. I caught the bus to London by myself and joined a group of twenty or thirty boys and girls with whom I was to spend the next month on the voyage to Australia.

4

A Sea Voyage

The gigantic warehouses of Tilbury appeared. Their sombre walls seemed to contain ominous secrets of our impending destiny. I suppose they were tired of departures and arrivals. They cancelled one another out in the end. Like dwarfs we invaded the enormous place. Our luggage was unloaded and we were herded through the church-like spaces to the wharf, where before our eyes the side of the ship rose vertically, cluttered with ropes, ladders, and steps. Soon, in single file, our hearts in our mouths, we were climbing the lurching gangplank to scale the enormous wall of the old liner, the *Balranald*. With lightened legs we trod the noiseless white planks of the deck. The narrow planks of scrubbed wood, their edges separated by black pencil lines, swept away like railway lines the whole undulating length of the ship. We went down into the bowels of the ship and were given our bunks, which were in cabins around the square of a hold. This square served as an assembly hall.

The child condemned to exile goes like a lamb from all he has known into the unknown, bemused by the novelty of his new surroundings. Feelings of apprehension are allayed by the urgency of adapting himself to new situations. The brilliantly clad ship's officers incline their heads to you and send you a smile as though they are your best friends. The sailors lift a non-committal finger to you. Three big funnels belch smoke. All the while, there is an uneasy feeling that you are being operated on by unseen hands that you cannot withstand or make aware that you are a living being with a mind of your own, which you would like them to understand. You are too small, too silent. The deaf hands go on doing what they want. They put before you another distracting scene, sever old loyalties and implant new ones.

The magnificent plain of the sea lay around our throbbing ship, its green surface breaking unexpectedly into foam. The heaving ocean would appear ominously before my eyes then disappear beneath me, leaving a watery valley in its place. The whole ship seemed alive and in its element, miraculously responding to the rhythm of the sea, buoyant like a bird. I had seen the gigantic furniture of the engine room, down whose fairy ladder I descended like a cripple. I had never seen anything working on such a colossal scale, or such a large single piece of metal, as the easily turning, silver, smooth propeller shaft. I wilted in the heat of the row of house-like furnaces. A man in dirty overalls opened the small door of one of them and threw in a shovelful of coal, holding himself back from the consuming mouth, whose red tongues played within. In Port Said, coal was carried onto the ship in wicker baskets, on the glistening brown bodies of Egyptians. I would have loved to join the line of great men serving this beautiful and powerful ship on which I uselessly stood, and which I inhabited like a dreamer.

The towering mass of Gibraltar, crowned with its great fort, symbol of the British Empire, rose before me one morning, yet it was a dwarf compared with what I had imagined it to be. I was very disappointed. Where did its divine authority lie? It looked ugly and diminutive. Around me the calm blue sea was ruffled by a light wind, and this dark, corrupt monster had to rise up out of that tranquil sea, into the ambrosial air, to spoil the first Mediterranean morning. I went from port to port, unable to accept the value man placed upon his own fatuous works.

At Malta the high brown walls stood before me, representing the rigid lines of the alien world I found myself in. Here was a barrier shutting me out from unknown human beings whom I desired to know. My ineptness as a social being sank into my heart. I was terrified of anything in human shape. I wanted to discover in them something that escaped that shape, but I was unable to join any of the little groups that formed among the boys my age. They seemed mostly bigger and more robust than I. Yet I was chosen by our guardian as leader, and I was proud of this title until I discovered no one took the least notice of me, and that I had virtually no one to lead but myself.

We were taken by the ship's boats to the quay at Malta, and there was the adventure of climbing a rope ladder down the ship's side. Swinging on the tenuous ladder I felt for the first time that my fate was in my own hands and, at the same time, what little ability I had to guide it. I had never felt so completely myself as when all my instincts came into play, swinging between the boat below and the deck above, like a leaf about to be blown from its tree. We formed in files on the ancient stones of the steep streets of Malta, and were guided through ornately decorated halls. I felt dwarfed by their high, vaulted ceilings and bewildered by their magnificence, but I remember with pleasure a flock of little white goats that were trotting down a steep street towards us on our way back to the ship. I had never seen such quaint and lovable animals, and the man driving them was equally lovable: a natural, happy human being, one of the first I had seen. He had a swarthy lined face and a very loose gait, and seemed more to be led by the goats than to drive them.

Although we were homeless orphans, we were treated like ladies and gentlemen on the ship, seated for meals at glitteringly laid tables, and waited upon by adults. By contrast, I think of the ant-like file of coal hauliers stoking the ships in Port Said, their thin, gleaming bodies all bent to the same shape by their wicker baskets. The impudent leviathans standing by the wharf swallowed countless thousands of those baskets. How could such monsters be kept alive by such diminutive beings? Only by their unquestioning service. This is what I admired about them and what made me want to join them. Slavery and guilt are one and the same. Happiness is irrelevant in an English education. I would not have dreamt of asking if these men who performed daily the arduous, repetitive task of hauling coal were happy. They seemed to embody what I had been taught life was — self-sacrifice.

Fear is intrinsic to living beings and makes it impossible for them to see how unimportant and valueless they are to nature. The only importance they have lies in what they give one another. Adults expect to be treated with respect for their importance by children but give none in return. Therefore, children become very fond of beings who do not expect importance, like animals, and the people of the East seemed to me to expect none. The dark people seemed not to need me, or to assume that I needed them. They were lovable for themselves, not like us white people who had to be loved for duties performed.

Among a group of boys where law does not prevail, the touchstone of one's esteem is the answer to the persistent question: who can fight? If you can beat everyone else in the group you are the real leader, no matter who has the title. I was certain I could not fight any of them, that even the smallest of my companions would get me down. My self-esteem was virtually non-existent and my appointment as leader only aggravated my despair. I clung more and more to a vanity in my appearance, that had been cultivated by my parents. I was the best looking of them all, I would deceive myself, and be well satisfied until my horrible vulnerability overwhelmed me. Then I would take comfort in the solidity of inert material things close to me. As spare as my physical contact with other human beings had been at home, it was more than the complete absence of human contact in my present environment, compounded by my own shyness.

What is a child looking for? Magical power. Something that is stronger than his father and mother. Stronger than the whole rational world to which he has to bend his will.

Every traveller assumes possession of his ship as we assume possession of the world. Many a lonely English boy has made a fetish of his ship, substituting contact with the inanimate for social contact.

The formless realisation that I had been abandoned grew and stirred in my soul. I was being irrevocably separated from home by increasing distance. Time and opportunity confirmed my belief that I did not know how to make a friend. I seemed unable to make advances, or initiate confidences. With those who offered a tentative friendship towards me, I grew cold. As a Londoner, I thought myself superior among a group of non-Londoners, but the source of my identity was disappearing forever. I escaped from this intolerable imprisonment in myself into nature, and into an infatuation with our guardian, a slender, very erect young Englishwoman with a wise face and gentle eyes. She seemed the embodiment of beauty and intelligence to me. Intelligence was a value that had always been stressed at home, but which I had never understood. Nature, to whom I had always resorted in my loneliness, taught me what beauty was.

I appealed to the broken surface of the bottomless ocean, whose sinister beauty fascinated me. Mist hung over the shore. With imperceptible motion, our great mother of a ship drew us with greedy eyes towards Colombo. Nature was unveiling her most beautiful land, the sun liberating her colours, forms and scents. On the wharf a tanned Englishman in white helmet and white suit was waiting to take us out for a day at the zoo. In the narrow carriage of a train we were jolted gradually upwards through profuse vegetation, whose intense green and voluminous waves intoxicated me, immersing me in the evidence of creation I wanted. Gigantic trees with great black trunks passed us by. Colour asserted itself here, never allowing itself to be forgotten in the object. Rivers of green ran into the eyes.

There seemed to be neither walls nor enclosure in the zoo. Lean grey monkeys examined us shyly from on high with wide open clever eyes, crying out like playful children, disappearing behind the walls of leaves and returning. Their self-effacement and soft curious glances forged a secret bond between themselves and me. A restless group of elephants was chained in a large open square and from one small eye poured down on me ages of patient suffering. A skirted brown boy smiled down at us from one of their backs. I flew up into his being with my bitterness. If a man cannot sense the cruelty of keeping an animal confined, how will he ever unburden himself of his prisons? The air of the zoo's gardens was still and heavy with scents. With pocket money I bought some sugar cane, and searched without success for its sweetness. One may spend one's whole life looking for oneself in other things, even forgetting oneself, to give life to inanimate things.

The longest part of the journey was now before us, Colombo to Fremantle. I was unable to escape the straitjacket in which my emotions had been strapped for longer than I could remember, an iron ring forged around my soul. I sensed I lived a makeshift life, reserving my real self for expression at some ideal future time. My stepparents had preserved me so thoroughly in their conventions, I could not destroy them. Thus I could not comprehend how boys could strip and perform lewd, naked dances together, such as I saw when I silently climbed the iron partition and peered into the big boys' cabin. I was excruciatingly embarrassed by my own and others' nakedness. My conscience insisted I inform our guardian of the atrocities the older boys were up to, but I was unable to find the words to do so.

The tilting boards of the ship eventually gave place to the dark monument of Fremantle wharf. It was early morning. The wharf was bare and the sea flat. The sun was already blazing in the clear air. A few brawny men were pushing trolleys around, disappearing in the vast sheds. In a group on the deck we children watched the ship's officers help rich old ladies and gentlemen down the gangplank. Impatient to tread the earth, we were restrained while the first-class passengers alighted.

A sinister emptiness and silence confronted me in the narrow dockside streets of Fremantle. The small houses and cobblestones were reminiscent of some vaguely recollected English village. In spite of the blazing sun, the street outside the docks where we waited for a bus to take us to the station had a depressing air, and the people looked glum and oppressed. With the little band of children I stood and waited. I hated them and the alien surroundings that separated me so certainly from home and city life. I stood alone, helpless and vulnerable among them all, in an uncharted country where I knew no grown-ups to whom I could resort for protection. I soon discovered that I had to obey orders to survive, and like a sheep, succumb to mob rule. Most of the other children had come from institutions, and did not find the regimentation so strange, but to me it was irksome and embarrassing, for in spite of my repressive life at home, I had never belonged to a group. I did not like giving orders or taking them. I had always walked alone.

I was still in love with the lady who had looked after us on the ship, and remained so long after she returned to England. She had only to smile at me for me to obey her. I was very miserable when I learnt that her place was to be taken by a severe faced military man with one arm, called the Colonel. In him I instantly felt the supremacy of brute force, and wilted into non-existence in his presence. His one arm tempted me to imagine he would be handicapped in the inevitable confrontation, but the illusion was soon dispelled by the stories of his superhuman strength. He had the wrath and strength of an injured animal, and could hold you like a vice with the stump of one arm while he beat you mercilessly with the other. The Colonel took charge of us as soon as we landed and our kind lady of the voyage became a dream.

5

Fairbridge Farm

The Colonel was very gentle with the girls, shepherding them out of danger or embarrassment or fear. But I could not hope he would sympathise with my radical unhappiness. His impersonal, imperious tone demanded obedience. I had been brought here to do as I was told, to be an indistinguishable member of a group, and to be deprived of the relatively immense freedom I had had at home in London. I dared not take a step here alone for I felt I had already mapped out in the London streets the physical conditions of my life, and could not begin again in a country so vast and trackless, so absolutely unknown.

With a benign smile transforming his stern features, the Colonel ushered us aboard a narrow railway carriage where we huddled together around him in one compartment to listen to him explaining our future life on the farm. His eyes twinkled as he foretold how our faces would be transformed into brown leather like his own. I tried to merge into the group hanging upon his words, but I only sank further into the space of myself, horrifyingly lost, disoriented. I clung to a strange new hope in fraternity. The train rattled along very slowly, the compartment congested with our small eager bodies, almost on top of the patient Colonel, who, no doubt, had made this same journey many times before. His figure almost filled the compartment, and I felt alarmed by his restless long legs. He seemed all limbs. As we moved further into the country, which sparkled under the bright sunshine, it became warmer and warmer, the heavy sun rising aloft, and I felt the tug of group bonds becoming stronger and my ego dissolving. There seemed such comradeship among our little group with the generous warmth of the Colonel at its head. But we had been sent out here to become domestic animals and I sensed an ulterior design in all the solicitude and togetherness. After all, I had been practising subterfuges myself for many years.

We got out at Pinjarra. The heavy-scented air was dry, fresh and intoxicating, not enclosing like that of the sea. The earth was spacious and empty but warm. The trees large and delicate and breathing a rapturous scent. There was a river that barely moved but looked old and deep. We sat by its flat broad expanse waiting for the farm truck. The hot sun beat down on our heads, and was reflected dazzlingly from tin roofs. The streets seemed immensely wide and completely deserted, and the houses with their large leafy gardens were widely and haphazardly scattered. The somnolent earth was undisturbed; it lay in a great silence. Our little company of thirty shrank into an insignificant presence in the enveloping primal space, packed with silence. I stared at the river and wondered.

The little wooden truck arrived and half of us were carried off in its back, precariously perched on our luggage, the gravel road flashing by. Some of the boys knew appropriate institutional songs and sang together loudly, while I sat in fear of opening my mouth and making a false sound. The essential difference between us was that they were able to join together as one spontaneously, while bourgeois pretence confined me in its torturing solitude. I had been told that I had a good voice, which meant a voice pleasing to my middle-class opera-loving parents. I was afraid of revealing my difference from the others, of singing too loudly, of being the object of derision or distinction from the group I wanted — for the first time — to join. I was afraid of seeming to be what I knew I was not. I divined that they would know that since I was five, I had not been what I was. Each of these sentences to solitary confinement, delivered by my adoptive parents, enlarged the abyss between my companions and myself.

I clung desperately onto the luggage to avoid being thrown over the side of the truck by the corrugations in the gravel road, which ran for miles through broad expanses of baking grass, and between high walls of forest. The rough-hewn jarrah fence posts carrying their four taut strands of wire ran past, proclaiming the jealous god of property whom we were to help appease. They were like their counterparts at home, the spiked iron fences, and broken-glass topped walls. We turned off the main road into the farm property and rushed along another perfectly straight road for two miles. The tapering grey skeletons of enormous dead trees stood on one side and a curving line of bowed trees, marking the course of a small river, on the other. We had entered the farm through the two-mile gate where there was really no gate but only two stout corner posts, and later on we passed through the half-mile gate, where again there were two stout posts with a wooden grill on the ground between them to stop the escape of cattle. Finally, we passed through a real gate, a ponderous wooden structure, which had been left open for us, into the residential area of the farm. This consisted of numerous dark weatherboard buildings each raised on thick posts set in the ground.

We were dropped off at the first of these buildings, the store, whose frowning aspect probably deterred many an impulse to rob it. Our luggage was dumped on the verandah and the truck dashed off to get those who had been left behind. Alien and helpless, like so many dumb domestic animals, we were now distributed to our cottages and new 'mothers'.

Fairbridge farm lay on a sandy, partially flooded plain at the foot of low, boulder strewn ranges, whose ridges rose one behind the other interminably, daunting the would-be truant. Cracked and flaked, huge grey boulders hung on the hillsides, and lay in a tumbled trail beside the waterfalls and pools of the narrow river. Here and there, the fallen trunks of giant trees lay partially burnt in their white and orange ashes. Between the hills and the cottages there was a mile or two of bush, where ancient gnarled jarrahs and tall white-grey gums were peopled by parrots and crows, and through whose airy palaces echoed the laughter of the kookaburras. Beneath the wide flung branches hid the fragile forms of fantastically shaped orchids.

With two small boys guiding me along the white sandy paths beside wide deep drains, I struggled with my large suitcase to Rhodes, my cottage, stopping repeatedly to recover my breath and the strength in my arms. My guides watched sympathetically. I eventually got my case up the wide wooden steps onto the bare polished floor of a spacious verandah, where I was met by a kindly old lady, Mrs Tomkinson. This was her private verandah from which doors led into her room and the boys' dormitory. I was to learn she attached great importance to the immaculate polishing of this verandah floor, as she did also to the dormitory floor. Both were polished with kerosene and their dark grain shone beneath a mirror-like surface, reflecting the hot summer light.

As the sun was going down over the forgotten sea, visible from the top of the first range of hills, I sat down in the dining room of the cottage for tea for the first time. The long wooden form was drawn up to the room-length table and filled with boys with Mrs Tomkinson at its head. Her fine silver hair and lined face cast a benevolent aura over the scene. I could feel the boys were fond of her, especially two or three older boys who were very tall and strong and seemed to go about with a perpetual stoop as though always on the point of listening respectfully to her wishes. Tea was the only meal taken in the cottage, and consisted of bread, treacle and cocoa. The other meals were taken in the dining room some distance away, where the whole school assembled under the surveillance of the Colonel, sitting at the head of the senior boys' table.

The rough concrete bath in the crowded communal bathroom was the revelation of my sin and punishment, my degrading exile made manifest. Brown and odious, the bath was to me like a grave. Like a corpse, I had to strip myself, exposing my shameful self to everybody's gaze. One cannot pretend when one is naked. I could hide in the dirty water from the dozen boys pushing and shoving in the narrow bathroom, but my partner in the bath was a mortal threat to my carefully preserved ego. It was impossible for our legs not to meet. Yet I found I enjoyed this contact under the warm water, and concluded it must be quite innocent, because my partner seemed unaware of it. The roughness of the bath against my skin constituted punishment for the irredeemable colossus of my guilt, which alone could explain this unimaginable rejection by my parents.

The bathroom was draughty, and on getting out of the bath this provided an excuse to bend over with an overt shudder, to hide my genitals until safely close to a corner, where I could unbend and dry my back. A battered dipper was used to transfer the water to the bath. The dipper appealed to me as a primitive functional receptacle, whose being remained unnoticed yet was indispensable. It and other things — like the cupboard for clean towels and pyjamas, the open fireplaces, the trestle tables of polished jarrah — proclaimed the indefinable unity of form and function that only individually made things possess. It called me back to the simplicity of the past, so buried in London.

Outwardly, I was submerged in the corporate life of the farm, while inwardly I suffered the perpetual torment of shyness and fear. I had never lived a domestic life among boys and I was afraid of them. I lost myself in nature, conversing silently with the new shapes of leaves, birds and lizards. I was drawn to the primeval grasstrees they called blackboys, whose tall slender spikes looked like a headdress concealing a spellbound native who would awake to help me face the dreaded world. But our job was to knock the magic blackboy over and smash up his resinous trunk for fuel, which we would put into a wheat bag and carry home to the wood heap and the kitchen. The bush was a mine of discoveries, wildflowers, orchids, parrots, ants, the dead logs, and at the same time provided an emptiness where I need not disguise my loneliness, and need not fear boys and men.

In the dawn, the lonely bugler would stand on the bare hill in front of the Norman church overlooking the farm, and turning towards the sleeping cottages, blow reveille with all his might, urging us out of our iron beds. We washed our faces in cold water, and then filed down the narrow, sandy tracks to the spacious weatherboard dining room. Like everybody else I went barefoot, despite possessing shoes, and had to suffer bruises and stubbed toes, one of the boys' common oppressions. Inwardly I seethed against the complacency with which long established communal behaviour was imposed on me. The very succession of events was tyrannical. On leaving the cottage our steps would lead in only one direction, towards the dining hall. Upon arriving there, we would, in an apparently automatic way, assemble around the prescribed table. This new phenomenon of order and sequence seemed to strike at me personally, and I made myself miserable revolting secretly and vainly against it, for I had expected to continue the aimless way of life I enjoyed in England. Nobody questioned the strict timetable. When three hundred boys and girls are performing as one, it is impossible to express oneself.

As soon as we were all sitting around our cottage tables, guessing at what was for breakfast, the Colonel, in his invariably grey suit, would come in with long strides from where he had been watching on the porch. Sitting erect at the head of the nearest table, he would keep silent until we all rose and were still. Then his imperious voice would enunciate the lord's prayer and grace with exaggerated clarity, while our mumbling accompanied him. With a loud clangour we would all sit down. Perhaps a form would fall over or an enamel plate would bounce on the floor. Those on duty would dash to the kitchen for the porridge, which they would bring back in a large dish and place in front of the cottage mother, who would ladle it into each plate, to be passed around in silence.

The notorious main kitchen was reached through an opening in the wall of the dining room. Through it could be seen the enormous black stove occupying the middle of the room, its wide chimney ascending among the dingy rafters of the roof. This stove was a tyrant whose weapons of oppression were grease and soot. After leaving school at fourteen, boys would be sent to work in the main kitchen for one or two months at a time. The place was so feared — largely on account of the man that ran it — that this assignment was like a prison sentence. The cook was a big cruel-faced man, with terrible long arms and heavy feet. He extorted slavish obedience with menacing gestures and words, and used the dirt and grease that unavoidably accompanied cooking to oppress and destroy the spirit of boys who were, with few exceptions, generous and co-operative. The size of the pots and pans sometimes exceeded their physical powers, and the grease and soot with which they were caked would have tried the patience of Sisyphus. But this kitchen god unrelentingly held his menials in his grip until the metal of every utensil was shining, sometimes keeping them there whole afternoons when they should have been resting, for they had to get up at four in the morning to prepare breakfast. Sometimes there was insufficient hot water to lather the soap, and one could stand at the trough for hours spreading the grease instead of removing it. This aroused the cook's ire and his voice would scald you with abusive insinuations, his big hands pushing you over.

Along the sandy tracks and roads between the cottages were the silent drains, cut, as with a knife, deep and straight in the grey soil and orange clay. After rain they carried turbulent muddy water. In spring they were clear rippling streams; in summer they were parched like the path that burnt my feet. The ravaged earth was a constant reminder of my guilt and terrible punishment; of my own inevitable death, swallowed up, dematerialised, for all those wrong-doings I'd ever been accused of. I found new, more creative reality, in the trees. Strong but peaceable towers, with undressed and tattooed bodies, and uncombed heads, their limbs danced out protectively, divertingly.

There was a big red gum leaning in one corner of the otherwise bare back yard, whose red, hard bark defied all dissections of boyish concupiscence, and whose heavy boughs twisted above the white earth with bunches of pregnant gumnuts in their glittering fingers. The fallen gumnuts made useful missiles with which we made contact with boys from other cottages. I would fondle the massive trunk of this tree as though its being were an affirmation of my own existence. Jarrah was my favourite tree because only the short and twisted ones had been left by the timber cutters, for they were used everywhere for railway sleepers. I admired its straight grain and pink wood. It burnt like coal. I sensed its value, coveted it, and always searched for its logs to drag or carry home to the wood heap, rather than the cross-grained white gum.

The school was on the edge of the bush, its small, low, dark buildings mottled by the shadows of the gum trees. To escape the stick was the motive for my school work, which I accomplished well enough, keeping the eyes of my bullying schoolmaster off me most of the time. Others were not so lucky and received terrible thrashings. The master would become possessed by his passion for striking writhing flesh and pursue a boy around the room making the cane whistle. Fortunately, he left those who could do the work quietly to themselves and a little knot of us competed in a back corner for firsts in maths and spelling.

There was amongst us a genial, open-faced boy who seemed to have affection to spare, and who easily surpassed the whole class in drawing. I remember my astonishment and admiration upon first seeing his drawing. It was a parrot's wing. Before the lesson was over he would have made a faultless and beautiful copy, using his pencil very lightly and without any sign of correction. This was my first meeting with natural talent and it carried the shock of the miraculous. What a fraud teaching was in the light of this miracle. A very studious mathematician sat just in front of me, his head bent over his book, staring through large steel-rimmed glasses. He never spoke and was never molested by the master. He would get every sum right, and always beat me to first place in maths. Like the artist, but in a much less sun-like way, he instilled in me an awe of inborn talent. You felt that that thick body and unremitting stare could solve every problem. Yet though I felt a natural affinity I could never get to know him. He was older and bigger, and something of a bear, and terror and shyness prevented any approach on my part.

The headmaster was a smooth-faced complaisant man. Always dressed in light grey, he seemed to wish to publicise the fact that he did not have to work, and moved from one part of the school to another as though exhibiting himself. However, he worked in the realms of the spirit. Upon coming face to face with him I would immediately feel guilty, as though he had discovered a hidden badness, or transgression of not only school rules, but of those unintelligible rules that only grown-ups, and only middle-class grown-ups, know and preserve. He was one of those men who invoke guilt by their very presence — they are so manifestly in league with what they conceive to be the almighty — and he had a way of looking at me that aroused feelings of imminent annihilation. I would search in myself for my wrong-doings and, finding none, assumed unknown ones to meet the headmaster's passion for sin. To please him, it was necessary to be guilty. In this he subverted the relations I was trying to develop with my new world, so that I wavered between that and submission to him. Our meetings were embarrassingly personal. Once he called me to his table in the room where he took the top class of girls. In insinuating tones, he accused me of levity with the girls, and of an incipient moral lassitude that would work my destruction. In pregnant undertones he warned me to alter my prurient and lascivious career, which he could see, and of which he could even intimate to me the reality, although I had no knowledge of it. Indeed, his language was unintelligible to me.

The headmaster persuaded me I needed his help and,

bewildered, I accepted his judgement. After I had finished my school days, I was allocated to work in the cottage where he lived with his wife. They had no children and were both devoutly religious. This duty was considered an enviable one, although I had to light the cottage stove and cook the family's porridge at seven o'clock every morning. After a year's experience of communal life, I became conscious for the first time of the insularity of family life. The headmaster and his wife lived in the community but outside it. They had their own house and garden. They were prepared to waste time which the community could have used fruitfully, demanding a boy work eight hours a day, five and a half days a week, on their small house and garden, which could have easily been kept by the wife, or in one or two hours a day by a boy. I began to learn how to waste time. I would let my mind go over a problem again and again, perhaps more for the pleasure of the logical operations than for coming to any conclusions. I was forced, in order to fulfil my duty, to keep my face to the earth for several hours a day, with no purpose but to satisfy the headmaster's dominion over me. I would dig the earth of their garden, pushing the spade irresolutely into the ground, row after row, just to make the slow hours pass, for I was never given anything to grow.

I had also to wash up, clean the kitchen and feed the fowls. I passed time in a small, dark shed where bins of feed were kept, inhaling the evocative scents of wheat and oats and turning the stiff handle of the grinder in which the wheat grains disappeared. No wheat grain was like another, but each one would give birth to all the others, if it alone were free. I would eat the wheat, cramming it into my mouth, vainly trying to know its wild taste. I would go back to the cottage with handfuls in my pockets for one or two of the boys, for this passion for wheat seemed to belong to a certain age only. I prized such gifts for they were all the communication I had with other boys, and saved me from both falling into the world of fearful intimacy and suffering from the lack of it.

I had begun to think about god and the universe, although god had never existed for me. The story of Christ became important to me and occupied my mind for several years. He was the ideal human being, the only focus of my affections, and the unending subject of my thoughts. The notion of god remained alien, in spite of regular sermons by eloquent English clergymen in the red brick chapel on the hill. I saw only the infinite material universe, and was unable to hold on to anything mystical. The clergymen appeared to me amusing storytellers. What appealed to me about Christ was his solid humanity and his acting humanely. This occupant of my head was my only friend during my boyhood. In his eyes was the prohibited love I wanted. Through him I became both the giver and receiver, and in his behaviour I suffered and recovered my lost gentleness. He held an extraordinary reality for me. He was never spiritual; I identified him with man. In church the choir looked like an assembly of Christs, dressed in their long white robes, their faces radiant with the effort of singing. All the devotion the church inspired in me I gave to Christ, to the memory of a living man, with whom anyone might have been on earth. I could not accept any beliefs that were not reasonable. It was possible for man to be Christ-like, therefore there was no need for any mystifying dogmas connecting Christ with god. Man was sufficient explanation of Christ.

Our church services were simple and powerful, with

beautiful singing accompanied by a resounding organ. The padre was held in reverence as a mediator for children in trouble with the Colonel or other authorities. He was probably the only educated man we had contact with, and only he could suspend the awful arm of the vengeful Colonel. The weekly sermon in good English revived vague memories of home. The padres themselves were usually fresh from England, for they did not stay long, and always seemed in a passion to impress a final memorable message on us, the permanent exiles. Some of these services were deeply moving, especially those in which the best boy sopranos sang solo. One of these, Sullivan, lived in my cottage. His voice had a bittersweet tone and would vibrate sonorously, penetrating the captured spaces, defying every attempt to describe it. It was another instance of the natural miracle of talent; instances that make one impulsively declare that talent is everything.

Sullivan had a countenance which immediately struck me with its open intelligence and impulsive generosity, not the kind that gives gifts, but which gives recognition, in large smiling blue eyes and a full wide mouth. He had a particularly engaging, self-effacing manner and was never ill-tempered. He was not tall, but robust, and was probably the oldest boy in the cottage when I arrived. But in spite of his gentleness he kept an inviolate distance between the young ones and himself, as though he were preserving them from a certain disillusionment that seemed to haunt him. When you approached him he seemed to deliberately withhold himself, and at the least excuse, would disappear. It was almost impossible to make him sing anywhere but in church, and he was not fond of church. A clean-cut figure, whose faded work clothes suited him well, he seemed to carry a load of fate around with him permanently, of which he was both the invincible warden and the helpless victim. I hated him for his aloofness, and loved him for his beauty. I think many a younger boy may have succumbed to the spell of his beauty, which may have necessitated his protective reserve.

I had no notion how to do anything practical, and would be fumbling over a task which other boys would finish as though they were born knowing how to do it. Demoralised by my inability to light the fire under the water heater, I was often pulled away by some disgusted boy or maddened adult from billows of choking smoke. I watched helplessly and penitently, hating my would-be teacher. Equally formidable was the business of chopping wood. The bedraggled wood heap was the theatre where I daily faced a number of challenges.

Adamantine logs lay like snarling dogs, their twisted shapes defying all attempts to loosen their knotty grain. Their flanks were hideously scarred with axe wounds. Spread around in a vast circle was a deep blanket of wood chips, giving purchase to one's curling toes. The long stemmed, heavy headed axe and short powerful iron wedges lay about on the chips. The long flat blade of the crosscut saw sagged over a half-divided log, its innocent looking teeth concealing dagger-like points and chisel-like edges.

Implicit in all the relationships on the farm was the trial of strength. The ultimate deterrent was corporal punishment, formal, or violent. It began at the top, with the explosive tempers and threatening fists of the numerous managers in charge of the dairy, the gardens, the kitchen, the drains, and other sections of the farm. It descended to the boys, who accepted it as a means of fixing their own position in the hierarchy. Bludgeoned into submission to perpetual hard labour by the rankling image of the descending fist, each boy imposed and maintained what dominion he could over his fellows with his own fist, converting his own shameful oppression into a vain tyranny. Like a slow vast whirlpool this tenor of violence absorbed everybody, so that, even among friends, fist fights decided issues of uncertain precedence. The exaggerated value placed on physical strength might be understood on the grounds that it was essential to the development of the country, which was still largely virgin, and where machines had yet made little intrusion. But this does not account for the pugnacious, anti-human form in which strength was conceived. It was construed, first and foremost as a weapon to control one's fellow men, not as a creative, productive power. Nothing is more grotesque, or such an anomaly in nature, than to see two boys or men fighting, and yet they quickly attract an interested, abetting audience. No matter how bloody the antagonists become, they are encouraged to continue until the audience is forced to accept the inevitable shamefaced end. The combatants, brought together by the evil genius of society, perform until they drop, exposing by their fruitless efforts the emptiness of the myth that they, together with all the audience, are living.

I was caught in this banal ceremonial twice: once with a boy with whom I maintained an unstable friendship, and once with an older, bigger boy. Neither I nor my opponents could fight. We were all cowards, taking up postures before each other to satisfy the invisible gods. I did not succeed in demonstrating my superiority to them, and they both obliged me to grant grudging deference to them. But none of this made us abandon obeisance to the law that might is right, and the image of the arbitrating fist was paramount in our mind. We had no notion of justice.

In time and with practice, I became fond of using the axe, and developed my embarrassingly small muscles. I enjoyed training my eye to strike accurately with the heavy-headed tool. Such accomplishments fed my self-esteem. The axe, with its long, smooth handle, and nerve-like grain, was like a wild animal in my small hands. It bounced off some kinds of wood like a ball, while it would drop through others like lightning. I would return to the intractable logs like a mule, and persevere until the rubbery surface yielded. I now found chopping very satisfying, training myself to reduce the number of strokes necessary to the minimum. It was exciting striking the nugget-like iron wedges into the cracks of stout logs with the back of the axe, rending them asunder as though with giant hands. The halves would fall apart with a hollow voice and an exultant ring of the released wedges and the scent of the tree would leap out. In the wood heap there was an approved and patent alibi for solitude, the cardinal sin of institutions. I could spend hours there, amassing a heap of carefully gauged billets, undisturbed, chopping to the accompaniment of self-nourished thought.

But when I broke an axe handle, the wood heap became my Gethsemane, for nothing was so symbolic of the farm's spirit, its underlying, inexplicit motive of ravaging and inseminating the virgin earth, as the axe handle. Such a catastrophe all too easily happens; invariably too violent a blow is delivered by the handle instead of the iron of the axe. The beautifully grained wood would shiver along its length, and split. Like Alice in Wonderland I would grow suddenly smaller, and wander like a penitent to ask the irate storekeeper for a new handle, and then, assuming the role of simpleton, ask one of the older boys to put it in the axe head for me.

One of the most repugnant duties was in the slaughterhouse. I was desolate at the thought of having to kill animals. Several sheep were killed a day, and one or two steers a week. The internal organs of the animals were fed to the pigs, which were penned in an enclosure close by. They lived in appalling conditions, and I could not understand why so intelligent an animal should be treated with so little respect.

Eventually my turn came on this odious job. The sheep to be killed was thrown with a single movement into a trough with its bewildered head over one end. It would try to right its head as though to take another look at the world, but it would be kept down by a hand on its face. In spite of my chronic anxiety over my strength, I was just able, by giving the sheep a vicious wrench with its wool, to hoist it on its back into the trough. This was considered one of the first steps in the graduation to man's estate. Another was to know which knife to take. The broad one was for skinning, the slightly narrower one for killing and the thin worn down one for finer detailed work. I made a clearing in the grey wool beside the ear, and drove the knife down into the neck. The stiff neck relaxed. Intelligence left the eyes. Blood ran over the fleece down onto the concrete. Beginners were not allowed to dress the sheep. I watched an older boy do this, feeling thwarted and disillusioned. If one can kill a sheep one ought to be allowed to attend to it afterwards.

Occasionally an unsuspecting steer would be led in, to be met by the manager with a pistol. He would put it calmly to the benign animal's broad brow. There was a pop and the colossal creature would collapse in a resigned heap onto the concrete, where we would watch, mesmerised with horror, its being skinned and disembowelled.

This fortunately brief apprenticeship to killing disturbed me. I thought I would never have the moral strength to accomplish it, and worse, I knew I did not have the moral strength to refuse it. My hands were innervated by my master's, and I hated myself for my treachery. Innocent animals were suffering the dreaded annihilation, and at my hands. I understood then that guilt and annihilation were not inexorably linked, that the innocent were also annihilated. I managed to avoid further killing by doing other duties associated with the slaughterhouse, like feeding the pigs with the internal organs. The pigs snuffed among them as though they were newly discovered roots, spilling the faeces out over their snouts, and snapping at one another with chilling obtuseness. It was not that I had a carefully grounded conviction against killing animals, but I identified myself with the animal and so felt I was killing myself. In this way, of course, I might have vicariously freed myself from guilt, and perhaps this explains why some slaughtermen are so proud of their skill. But I did not want to relinquish my guilt. It was the secret source of my power.

My term in the dairy too only served to lower my opinion of myself. The cows literally kicked my goodwill back at me, putting their hooves in the bucket that I held like a beggar beneath their tight little udders, resting them with exasperating composure on my bare toes, and kicking me off my stool. My demoralised state was pretty much constant, and I escaped it only when I left the farm at fifteen, to go out to private employment.

In certain people we recognise ourselves, and these are the ones we least like to recall. This has nothing to do with physical resemblance. It is one of character and destiny perhaps. The person I am thinking of was so ordinary and undistinguished a boy that it is embarrassing to describe him. He was shy and retiring, with a disquieting manner, as though he were unsure of your intentions towards him. He seemed afraid, but nevertheless ready to spring like a small wild animal if you molested him. This boy was Perrins, and he and I maintained an ambiguous friendship for the three years I was at the farm. He was even less at home in the bush than I, and here I could, unchallenged, take the leading role. Others must have recognised a connection between us for, when two boys were assigned to a duty, as for example, to wash after tea, he and I were invariably put together. This seemed natural to us, in a way that we were never able to articulate. Our bond was emotional and inarticulate. Perhaps we were looking for the same thing, atonement for perennial guilt. Perrins had an elusive, almost sly personality, with a facile smile. It was impossible for me to really touch him, although I often felt a love for him. There was some deeply buried barrier between us, and he often abused my affection with wilfulness and a want of seriousness. He was attractive when formally dressed, exhibiting above his white collar and striped tie, a large swarthy countenance with asiatic cheekbones and a ready oriental smile. He was a choirboy and impressive in his white cassock, his large pointed head bowed over the reverently held hymn book. But the whole picture was set awry by an air of diffidence, which always accompanied him. He was always elsewhere. We never spoke about our past. It constituted an inveterate unconscious obstacle to any mutual understanding.

Very different was Ostwald, a solidly built boy who spoke so softly, he seemed always to be disclosing a secret. At any attempt to persuade him with your opinion, he manifested an aversion bordering on hatred, and withdrew behind a smooth armour. He was very domesticated, and enjoyed duties that most boys avoided, like getting stores, and making cocoa, even polishing floors, the most obnoxious of jobs to most of us. He would swing his heavy back over the reflecting surface with audible satisfaction. But he was lazy when it came to outdoor work, and was willing to leave chopping and gathering wood to others. He walked with the air of a man of substance, proud and seemingly without fear and yet there was a feminine softness about him.

I wanted to influence Ostwald for I imagined my education superior to his. I was successful in school, where he was continually in trouble, reputed a dunce and persecuted by the teacher for his stolid, immoveable stance. The teacher would thrash Ostwald with the cane, beside himself with ugly red-faced temper. Ossie wouldn't make a sound, receiving all the blows like a rock. I affronted him with my bookish evangelism, and fuelled by his pride, there grew a wall between us. However, Ostwald was friend to us all because he knew how to make the cottage more homelike.

I was jealous of Ostwald's popularity. The same age as me, he was my rival for precedence among the smaller boys, so I picked a quarrel with him. He was very obstinate, and we fought on the large verandah of the cottage, barracked on by the younger boys. An older boy would have stopped us. I could not reach his face. His arms were heavy and long and easily kept my contemptible attacks at bay. I was demented by benighted passion, but cowardly and frightened of getting hurt, and he was as solid and immoveable as ever. I was filled with desperate hatred and despair. He gave me a terrible blow on the nose, and then another, as though with a hammer. I became dizzy, and my nose was filled with blood. Abject, I sank onto a form by the wall, Ostwald standing quietly by, untouched. Everyone dispersed in shameful silence. I felt subdued from my conceited height to futile smouldering rebellion.

There were boys of my age who had been at the farm for several years, and were adept little bushmen. They were much keener sighted than I, and when we went looking for orchids, one of them would always pounce before me. Under the curving jarrah branches, under a blue sky, we scoured the sparsely covered dry earth for undiscovered phenomena, the radiant, gold cowslip orchid, the opulent brown and yellow donkey orchid, and the shy enamel orchid that echoed the blue of the sky. The miraculous likeness between the flowers and their namesakes, the long legs of the spider orchid, the horns of the snail orchid, the long ears of the donkey orchid, the placidity of the cowslip orchid, seemed almost deliberate imitation.

Occasionally, we were diverted from the ground by a lightning flight of newly painted parrots. An English boy has never seen a parrot or, perhaps, a many-coloured bird at all, and suddenly, in this unknown country, he sees rainbow-like meteors slipping through the branches of white gums.

What excitement to find the eccentric smokebush, when one is not sure whether the white fluff is really enchanted smoke, or the blue of leschenaultia, and king of all plants, the majestic grasstrees. What a mine for the heart is the West Australian bush: hot, dry, colourful, scented, infinitely cunning and infinitely gracious. It was the bush that reared the bushman, the man mysterious to all Europeans, content to live alone within its depths. One day, he is found by an inquisitive stranger from the northern hemisphere, gone from the earth of his body. That stranger doesn't understand the meaning of a life spent totally, deliberately, away from civilisation. To him, the bushman is just a freak, a madman. One day perhaps, the stranger will see the bush is all he needs.

At Fairbridge, the bush was my only joy.

6

A Brief Freedom

On the back of the little worn out truck in which I had been brought to the farm, I was taken into Pinjarra Station. Shaken along in the box-like compartment of the train, watching the red and green kangaroo paws slip by the track, I easily allowed the chains of the past three years to fall away, and held my freedom to me like a prize. In a Perth store, I moved blindly to and fro collecting my new clothes. The cottage mother who had come to supervise insisted on my taking every item of the regulation list of clothing, while I, magnanimous in my new freedom, protested at receiving so much. Then a new interminable train journey began, over steep rocky hills into the flat limitless space of the inland, my new case on the rack opposite me, keeping the secret of my unworn clothes and boots. The engine burst with steam, climbing over the cuttings in the boulders of the hills, assailing my lungs with pungent smoke, and my cheeks and eyes with stinging soot, the persistent rattling and swaying tuned to my impatience. In the middle of an empty plain we would stop inexplicably until an oncoming train rushed by, or would remain stationary, gasping beside a water tower for ages while the engine filled up. In the night we stood for hours in sprawling stations that rose uncannily in the midst of vast plains. I stared bewitched at the looming shapes of sheds and towers which seemed raised on an enormous scale, as though for the commerce of giants. Occasionally, I heard the tread of an invisible railwayman, or the train would give a violent lurch, raising one's expectations of continuing the journey.

As dawn approached the cold increased, and I tried to sleep on the hard seat, muffled in a futile blanket. Suddenly the dewy windows sparkled in a blaze of light and the warm rays of the sun entered the compartment. Sleep was impossible, and sitting up, I gazed at the monotonous fences and telegraph poles, enjoying the warmth penetrating my stiff limbs.

Eventually, in the afternoon, I arrived at my goal, a tiny station in the midst of an apparently unpeopled country. I alone alighted on the dirt platform, handicapped by my suitcase, and the train immediately resumed its indifferent way. An immense silence and profound peace enveloped me. No one was there to meet me, and I felt contented to remain standing where I was, letting my vision accord with the enormous spaces, my soul snatching their promise of freedom. I seemed projected into space.

Soon enough a car drove up, and I was greeted in a friendly way by a big man in shirtsleeves, apologetic because his brother, my boss, had been unable to meet me. His wife was in the car. She was a beautiful woman. Her round arms were bare and there was a friendly smile on her face, the first time a woman had smiled at me for three years or more. She seemed completely free and I felt the attraction and promise of her freedom. The opposite sex had been taboo at Fairbridge. One was not permitted to talk to a girl, and it was a heinous offence to enter the girls' cottages. This proscription of mixing with the opposite sex, common in institutions, seems to me a deliberate attempt to thwart social development. Perhaps from there, it found its way generally among the youth of the working-class, who were excessively male oriented. The young couple dropped me at the farm house. I never saw them again, nor did I ever see my employer during the two or three weeks I was at the farm.

Life is only what one can remember and I remember so little. I deposited my heavy case in a wooden hut behind the farmhouse. Here I was shaken awake from the dreams that had accompanied my journey by the reserved welcome I received from the other three labourers who occupied the hut. Night was falling and a kerosene lamp, whose light was half obscured with soot, illuminated their faces. They seemed surprised that their little room should be expected to house me too, and looked about diffidently for a bed. There was a stretcher made from sacks sewn onto poles, which they had used as a basket, and they pointed this out deprecatingly to me. I eagerly assured them it was as good a bed as I expected. One man was mending his clothes and continued concentrating on this. The other two stared at me with wide appraising eyes as if assessing my strength and experience, making me painfully conscious of my complete lack of both. They were all very quiet and asked me questions in kind, soft tones.

The youngest of the three men was to be in charge of me, and in the following few days cruelly exposed my weakness, slowness, and ignorance of common farm practices. Like most youths who had worked on farms since leaving school, he was extremely quick and adroit at completing every job. He could milk six cows while I milked one. He could carry two hundred pounds while I could not lift a hundred. He could harness a horse in his sleep while I did not know one piece of harness from another. They were also extremely loyal to their masters, and, I suppose, I was not behind in this respect.

Now that I had left Fairbridge, an event looked forward to with impatience ever since turning fifteen, I conceived myself to be a free man. Infatuated with this imaginary freedom, I was all the more ready to put on any chains an avaricious farmer had waiting for me, turning these, with my show of ability and loyalty, into badges of independence. I wanted to succeed in doing something alone after being jealously supervised for the previous three years. There is an immediate sense of freedom in using our muscles and reason, our strength and skill. We are satisfied with this until we are worn out, and wonder where all the work of our hands has gone.

In the hut at night, its features softly outlined by the kerosene flame, its occupants seated on their beds musing or reflecting, my terror of men paralysed my tongue. I shunned the all too glaring intimacy, feigning fatigue in my makeshift bed. Thus I would go to sleep and awake with the same constriction of my heart. These men would probably have helped me had I been able to ask, but had often only to rescue me ignominiously. The almost physical pain of shyness and fear made the development of working relationships impossible, and the men must have quickly made it known to the boss that I could not do the work he had engaged me for.

There were two pig pens, one for those shortly to be slaughtered, and one for the numerous younger ones. I would enter the pens twice a day to feed the pigs, and thought I could win their affection with food but they were too hungry to worry about where it came from, and would all but knock me over in their struggle for it. Still, I enjoyed the task because they so obviously enjoyed their food, and I'm sure, as with all other jobs, I took far longer over this one than was allowed.

The pigs would look at me with reproachful eyes, as if trying to make me understand they were not made for such captivity. I understood all too well, for I did not see my position as different from theirs. This is what perhaps made it all the more distressing to see them slaughtered. For was this not also my fate: tainted from the beginning with iniquity, the only perfect requitement is death.

It was soon plain to me I was found wanting in both experience and strength. Nobody was unkind, but I felt they were at a loss as to how to employ me. Successively easier, soul-destroying jobs dragged me lower and lower in self-esteem. Tramping after an old draught horse, I spent hours pulling an ancient cart over the clods of a ploughed paddock, picking up dead roots and throwing them in the cart. The horse seemed long resigned to treading up and down the dusty furrows, pricking his heavy ears to my tentative noises and observing me with a pitying baleful eye. Then I would lead the unwilling horse across the furrows, undo his straps, and tip the cartload onto heaps built up in former years. The tedium made my heart shrink and filled my head with despairing thoughts. I would stretch out the time I spent splitting firewood for the homestead kitchen. The wood was very tough and I suppose I cut very little for the time I spent on it. Speed seemed to be the one desideratum.

My deepest source of shame was my incompetence with the separator, in which the kerosene tin of milk I was only just able to haul up the hill was poured every morning, to separate cream from milk. The separator's innumerable strangely shaped parts baffled me. I was not even allowed to wash it up for fear I might put it back together wrongly. My milking was slow and faltering and my young mentor, though he never showed any impatience with me, was no doubt himself impatient to get away to more interesting work. He found himself tied to rescuing me from incompetence.

I envied the teamster with his row of beautifully built horses coming home in the dusk to the silver chimes of harness, his day-long experience of noble work universally admired. First up in the morning, he was gone before I arose.

We ate on the back verandah of the homestead, looking out over the cleared valley below and the far hillside of bush. Our food was put in front of us by a young working girl in an apron who was from Fairbridge farm too, and on the basis of this bond, I immediately calculated we would fall in love. She would end my loneliness and make this alien place my home. But she made it clear after our first greetings that all her time belonged to her employer.

It was not long before I was again waiting on the siding for the train, audible in the distance, but out of sight. Where to now? I had no say in where I was sent to work. Fairbridge would be my legal guardian until I was twenty-one. The farmers contacted Fairbridge when they needed someone, and there we had to go. If you were really unhappy somewhere, you could ask to be sent to another job, but still you had no say in where that would be.

7

Tenterden

I got out at the little station of Tenterden and was met by a young man with the fairest complexion I had ever seen. In spite of my fear, I liked him and could not help responding happily to his broad smile. He carried off my case and I followed him to the large dusty car. We drove through miles of dreaming bush, while my shyness struck with redoubled force beside my new master's friendliness. At a high timbered gate between a neat weatherboard cottage and rough-hewn sheds, I got out to open my way into what I foresaw, with rankling despair, was my new slavery. Before me stretched a sea-like expanse of earth and, incalculably far in the distance, lying uniquely on the flat horizon, were fairy-like mountains, the Stirling Ranges. They remained there, monotonously calling my chained legs day after day. Cows and sheep peacefully grazed in nearby paddocks.

In a small cottage adjoining the house I met my fellow workman, Jack, who virtually managed the farm. The master was a gentleman whom I saw only on special occasions like shearing and harvest time. Jack and I had a little room each, which had been the master's rooms when he was a boy, evident in the pile of old school books that he had prudently kept. I was amazed at the beauty and intelligence set out in the carefully covered pages. He seemed a superior person and I felt lucky to have him as my master. I felt more at home here, and at weekends began reading mystery stories that he had also preserved from the past. I saw myself as the great detective.

The working man is in a continual state of revolt. He is said to have no soul; forced to hide it by those who make this judgement; forced to pretend he is indifferent to ownership of the land, and to what those who own do to it. Work has to be done. It is difficult to trace the value and destination of its fruits. The alarm clock would break my sleep in the dark early hours of the morning and, half asleep, my consciousness would mingle with the gloom, reaching for the blurred outline of a cow, as saviour of a despairing loneliness.

The cows were spread out in the watery, misty paddocks rising from the creek, unwilling to move until you approached them personally. Without family, in the country animals are one's only real friends. Individual animals will be suited to one's own disposition, and they seem to acknowledge friendship after a while by waiting upon your arrival and attention. The small herd of cows would be assembled before the milking shed and with their patient waiting, oblige you, despite your deep-seated feeling of revolt, to milk them.

To my relief, Jack put together the separator, whose complexities still evaded me, and separated the cream, while with an enormous broom I scrubbed the concrete of the stalls. I took a pail of milk over the slippery grass to the kitchen of the house, where I had the lowly duties of lighting the fire and washing up. The blazing sun would begin to ferment the day. The birds would cease to sing. Jack would leave the separator for me to dismantle and wash. Eventually I was able to put it together and come up to the house with the can of cream, which he would take to the station in the sulky later. Then we would both retire, well satisfied, to our cottage to wait for breakfast. A similar ritual would be repeated in the evening, the sun withdrawing its light as we were milking, gone by the time we washed and combed our hair for tea. It was a wondrous sight to watch Jack combing his hair. He would rub brilliantine in and sweep it back from his forehead with such a flourish of well-being and magnanimity.

One of my duties after completing the housework was to get a cartload of firewood if we were running short. The wood heap was again one of my purlieus. A benign old mare called Mary would remain motionless while I fumbled with her harness, her dark eyes looking down on me with disquieting detachment. I was afraid of her great shaggy hooves, but she soon enlightened me that she would lift them off the earth only when she could not avoid doing so. While I was solving the puzzle of the straps over her big hindquarters, she would flick me in the face with her tail in a friendly way. I would back her massive and reluctant body into the shafts of the cart, which I could just lift, and attach the cruel chains to the collar round her shoulders.

I would walk timorously beside the cart possessed by a nightmare of accidents, the tough leather reins in my hands like a diploma that would set all right. It seemed as though there were parts of the earth where the trees had come to die, for I twisted the horse through desolate gatherings of grey, bare trunks and limbs. Leafless branches rose into the sky and barkless trunks of colossal girth stood on the maimed earth like incomprehensible monuments. The whole panorama reflected my own barren hopelessness. How many years must pass before all that dead wood dissolved in the restoring soil, and living trees again reached for the sky? Perhaps men would have to depart first.

Getting a load of wood was an opportunity for me to get out in the wild by myself, away from my unassuaged fear of men's violence, away from the painful consciousness of my feeble and ignorant self, which the sight of men aroused in me. I would sit down on a dead branch and think about the origin of things, protracting my time away as much as possible, the old horse standing patiently by, the naked boughs of the dead trees bent over me.

I took my loneliness, my revolt against my menial position, and my shame at my relentless dependence into the bush and mulled over them as I picked my way over the refuse of dead wood and stones. I was exploring a novel earth where nature was prodigal of creation and destruction, unifying them here, where fallen trees mingled with the living, and barren rocks with prolific soil. Form sprang out of chaos before me. Beside this paddock preserved in its primitive shape, was one levelled by man, where the earth was grazed bare of its planted European grasses by sheep. The soil was beginning to flow away down shapeless gullies. A new galvanised iron windmill brought water from far beneath the soil, only to run quickly off the denuded earth. One of my duties was to attend to this lonely musician of a windmill, to see it kept the sheep supplied with water. I was fascinated by its spinning sails, so responsive to the wind, and the regular rhythm of its shaft, privy to the secrets of the earth.

Coming upon the shambles of an abandoned humpy my childish scavenging habit took possession of me and I peered among the grimy relics of the hermit for a prize. I found a pair of raw-hide soles for my boots, and carried them proudly home to show them, like proof of importance, to Jack, for the soles of our boots were always wearing thin. Even such a paltry aggrandisement offered an increment in self-esteem for one who had till now rarely helped himself to any of the world's goods, but imagined he had a right to them all.

The boss's wife, who imposed an officious and finicky rule in the kitchen, was nevertheless kind and sympathetic towards me, and when her two daughters came home from boarding school she asked me to come with them for a picnic. Alarmed though I was, I could not refuse. The four of us set out in the hot sun up the steady incline to the brow of the hill overlooking the property. There we sat among dry twigs in the shade of tortured gum trees, strained by our contradictory relationship of master and servant. Disconcerted by this false comradeship and embarrassed by my inability to respond to their overtures, I sat staring at the enormous expanse of earth, and the tiny house of our nearest neighbours on a distant hillside. I collected dead branches and, painfully conscious of my reputation for bungling such practical tasks, began building a fire for tea. The boss's wife unpacked her homemade cakes. The brilliant sun, warm breeze, and fecund earth thawed the estrangement between us a little, but I could not overcome my fear of their authority. Surrounded by the vast spaces of earth, my heart expanded with its spontaneous love of freedom, only to be abruptly checked by the tightening chains this little group of human beings bound themselves in. The boss's wife had sympathy for my helpless situation, and her two girls offered their friendship, but it was impossible for me to negotiate the dark, formless abyss that separated our two classes. I was in the false position of pretending to do things out of friendship that I was forced to do as a servant. It was impossible for me to express my natural kindness although I could not escape enjoying theirs.

On the way back, we gathered mushrooms in the broad, richly-manured paddock. I felt a compulsion to do something to exonerate my ingratitude, and looked frantically for the delicacies that my superiors so incomprehensibly loved.

Sunshine soaked the earth and the tender wheat stalks turned stiff and gold. The fluid paddock of wheat carried the wind across its surface. Beyond the further wall of the wheat sank the ragged pools of a trickling creek, under whose sheltering trees I searched vainly for crayfish. The perforated banks, submerged in the pure water, seemed unoccupied, when suddenly one's eye would catch sight of a pair of clumsy looking nippers. I offered my piece of fresh meat on a string, and they immediately withdrew. A pair of thread-like feelers took their place and, following a lightning-like dash at the meat, the canny animal drew back, not to be enticed out again. Jack would bring home half-a-billy-full, which he would boil and eat. I was amazed at the composure with which he devoured so many animals.

At harvest time the boss drove the harvester with three draught horses, while Jack took the horse and cart after them, taking off the bags of wheat. I collected the cut, rifled stalks, tying them into sheaves. Later, I raised the sheaves into tentative stooks, and soon could survey my little golden pyramids all over the razed paddock. The sky was full of dust. The echoing call of crows fell through the torrid air, and mice scampered for cover among the stubble. Clothes were soon drenched in sweat, and the horses' heads sank lower as the day lengthened and they repeated circle after circle in the high-headed wheat, toppling its ranks. Night would be quickly gathering by the time we went to milk the cows, who were chewing close together, waiting stock-still before the bales.

Jack was a strong, self-confident boy of eighteen, a farmer's son. He was unconscious of his strength and his self-confidence was natural, without arrogance or conceit. His face broke easily into a warm smile and his eyes were always laughing. I felt his sympathy and happily noticed his friendly attitude, for I was still in short pants, small and weak for my age. Yet I strained to keep up a pose of equality, while inside I was oppressed by my sense of inferiority. My chronic terror of men made me painfully tongue-tied in his presence. I suspect my heart was full of nothing but hatred. Jack seemed to love his employers and would do anything for them. But who could love someone who has control over them? He did a lot of my share of the work, for he accomplished the various jobs in less than half the time I would take. He went to bed early after tea while I read in the dim light of a kerosene lamp. At five in the morning the clamour of the alarm clock would wake me from a deep sleep. I would fumble to light the lamp while Jack was already dressed; stumble down to the milking shed while he was already far out in the damp, cold paddock, collecting the scattered, grazing cows. I was very slow but Jack never betrayed any annoyance; he worked with such nonchalant ease.

Shearing time was another occasion when I saw the boss working. He had a reputation as a good shearer. Neighbours came over to help him and the row of doubled-up bodies remained against the wall of the shearing shed all day. They used pointed steel clippers, which I could barely close, their blades rubbing one another with a resonant sound. The sheep's grey coats would fall before their points onto the floor, revealing white fleece, like waves unfurling into foam. Each shearer had his own pen of sheep, the shorn and the unshorn mixed together in a restless mass. Into this I would press myself, to clutch at their wool and pull them out to the impatient shearers who leaned over the inverted, unresisting animals, undressing them of their thick coats with sweep after sweep of their untiring shoulders. Stains of crimson blood would suddenly appear on the snowy fleece and sometimes bare flesh lay exposed. The shearing would go on remorselessly. The stoic sheep bore it with indifference, but when released ran off with tremulous complaints.

The closely woven, neatly folded wool sacks were unfolded in the cell-like wool press and filled with the pungent balls of wound up fleeces. I would prance top-heavily in the wool sacks, wedging the wool down the sides of the bale, so that often I thought I should not be able to extract my foot. The efficacy of the wool press filled me with admiration. Being ignorant of mechanics, its effective compression of the elastic, seemingly incompressible wool, I found miraculous. Emulating Jack, I alternately pulled the press's two iron pipe levers down, listening to the clock-like ticking of its ratchets. When my strength failed Jack would rescue me from my frustration, completing the sculptured bale; fastening it up with dexterous attacks of the bale hook.

Our two neighbours, both rough diamonds, sheared with ostentatious speed and I was repelled by their callous treatment of the helpless animals. They frequently wounded them with their thoughtless shears, in contrast to the boss who sheared with studied slowness, releasing sheep without a scratch and a perfectly smooth, new white coat.

One weekend Jack drove me in the buggy to see the boss playing in a local football match. A sprinkling of people dawdled around the white rail surrounding the ground, and farmers' wives began serving cakes and cups of tea in the small club house. I could not bring myself to go and get anything; the afternoon seemed a social occasion for landowners. The boss was the star of the match, springing head and shoulders higher than anybody else. He filled me with admiration. The eyes of the small crowd by the rail were riveted upon him, and I could feel the pleasure they all found in watching him. From the cradle he must have been made aware of his talents and beauty and this awareness did not desert him, even when he was castrating lambs with his teeth. Jack and I had to leave the game early for the seven-mile trot home to milk the cows.

On four sides of a perfect rectangle, about as large as a basketball ground, the orange gravel and clay of the baked earth rose steeply from a flat panel of muddy water. Several such dams were gouged out of the earth to relieve the dry summers. This one was in a treeless paddock usually inhabited only by sheep. The water was unruffled by the wind and remained icy cold long after the winter, in spite of the sun bearing down overhead. I fancied that a regular dip would improve my poor physique, and shuffling my feet in the slime of the bottom, I would not get out until I had swum at least once across the dam. Then, shamefaced, I would clamber like a cripple up the rough dam wall to catch the salve of the sun's last rays. Naked on the brow of the dam, apprehensive of being discovered, and subject to violent spasms of shivering, I would struggle to pull my clothes over my wet skin. Walking home, warmth suffused my limbs, and courage my mind, at having accomplished one independent action in my monotonously dependent existence.

8

Perth

I jumped over the netting fence to get the football Jack and I had been kicking to each other to pass the time of a Saturday afternoon. Returning, I attempted to leap the fence again and the heel of my heavy boot caught in the netting. I crashed into the earth and heard a sound like the breaking of a green bough from within my arm. I screamed with pain. The world seemed to have turned upside down. My tears began to flow. Jack tried to raise me up, then went to get the boss.

While I sat on a kitchen chair the boss had brought out onto the verandah I wondered, as the pain subsided, at the novel situation in which I found myself: receiving his and his wife's solicitous attentions, instead of their demanding mine. I saw that my accident immediately reversed our roles. While he fussed around me, the boss sent his wife to look for brandy. Jack stood helplessly by.

Inequality in possessions too easily establishes authoritarian relations between men and this prohibits them from showing signs of affection for one another. The boss had always held himself aloof from me, almost demonstrably so, I thought, but as soon as he saw my plight, I felt the strength of his sympathy and even affection.

Holding my arm gingerly, I sat on the soft leather of the front seat of his car, watching the gum leaves fly by as he drove me to the hospital, twenty miles away. The gravel road was empty and the brown dust swirled up behind us. We sat in silence. I could not think of anything to say though the boss repeatedly asked how I was. I felt myself a different person after the shock; a stranger to myself.

At the hospital I was left with reproachful haste by the boss, lost in a white linen turbulence of nurses. The doctor, a tall, slim, young man, like a god concerned over one of his broken creations, stood over me and examined my arm without speaking, murmuring incomprehensible phrases to the nurse behind me. I screamed while he relentlessly tugged at my arm, conscious intermittently of his eyes arraigning me and passing shameful judgement. I felt his annoyance. I felt guilty of some unfathomable crime. The doctor tugged in desperation and I screamed without pause. Eventually, it was over, my arm was swathed in plaster and I was put to bed.

A variety of magazines had collected in the hospital and I indulged my love of reading. I infused with life the paper heroes and heroines, bereft as I was of love and friendship, and a passion grew in me to learn about women's bodies, for I had never seen a naked girl or woman. Their hidden anatomy became a chronically teasing mystery and an ideal woman gradually took form from the ever rising smoke of the magazines' romances. I was seventeen.

My broken arm was so ill-set that I had to go to Perth to see an orthopaedic surgeon. I had lost the feeling in my fingers. My injury was giving me an air of importance, and I got a room at the YMCA. Walking alone through the drab streets of Perth, I was confused by conflicting feelings of being free from control for the first time in my life, and being abandoned. I had to meet the boss's father so that he might finalise the insurance for my injury. He was a very big man, who leaned over my small frame with a benevolence that made me blush and sweat, and for which in spite of my longing to do so, I was unable to thank him. I was mesmerised by the blank walls of the city and awe-struck by the gigantic interior of the insurance building. The motor cars seemed aimless and the streets colourless and dirty. I had wandered into a vast, meaningless, speechless canyon, stripped of nature's familiar assurances: the song of birds, the rustling of trees, the warmth of animals. I sought in vain to find acknowledgement of my existence in people's faces. The objects behind the shop windows seemed to bespeak more comradeship than the crowd that flowed by like a natural phenomenon. Still, the city was increasing my feeling of self-importance.

I had now to find my doctor, who was in St Georges Terrace, a wide, relatively pleasant thoroughfare. The impressive front of the leaning buildings and the austere comfort of the doctor's apartment further nourished my vanity. I had never before spent a day sitting idle, and began to enjoy the whimsical moods of the waiting room. The doctor was a tall, stooped, woman whose countenance was memorable for its rapid change from severity to kindness. She was obviously a lady. She spoke to me as though I was an equal, and I felt with her I might exercise my independent intelligence and be listened to. In fact she obliged me to be more independent and confident. I became very fond of her, but as ever, my shyness kept me tongue-tied in her presence. I felt dull and obtuse and was convinced I had disappointed her, simply because I was unable to express the tumult of feeling and emotion she aroused in me. Most of all, I was grateful to her for treating me as a human being. I loved entering her room. I felt a natural affinity for the medical world and had become very interested in physiology, although I had got no further than studying a nursing text book I found in the hospital.

She sent me to a small private hospital near King's Park. The radiologist, a friend of hers, moved me with the concern he evinced for my arm, of whose serious derangement I was unaware, and flattered me with the respectful way he talked to me. My surroundings had suddenly become unimaginably urbane. The hospital was like a private hotel, with a wide porch where convalescent patients lounged. The matron took me under her wing, and I straightaway began to feel that uneasiness that sincere affection evokes in me. I, who most needed love, withdrew from it in alarm. The matron was an able energetic woman who, although middle-aged, had never married. She enveloped me with the solicitude of a mother. Her dominating personality made me anxious for my independence, for I had been free from family ties for many years, and my thoughts and feelings were my own. However, I was elated at finding myself daily surrounded by women, and there was a tacit agreement that I should help the matron with the menial duties of the hospital in return for her care of me while I was in Perth. Although I grew fond of her, I found these domestic duties, stoking the boiler and washing up, irksome, reminding me of my place in England, where I had been virtually my parents' servant. I found myself again torn between the contradictions of love and hatred; hatred of obedience even to those I would love for their own sake. I writhed under orders and requests that could not be refused.

I loved the matron of the hospital while I depended on her to intervene between me and the void of the city. I hated her for her exercise of authority over me. She used my assumed love or gratitude to force me to work. Certainly the most menial tasks were all I could do in the hospital, but they were nonetheless oppressive, especially as I was just gaining some degree of independence within my servitude on the land by my slow mastery of its techniques.

Matron belonged to an Irish family and lived with her grandmother, her father, and her younger sister in their large house next to the hospital. It was obvious that she liked me and an affection for her grew in me, so that one of the few occasions when I have prayed was when she was seriously ill with pneumonia. The old grandmother had the genteel dress and friendly manners of another world, and a silent authority that no one questioned, slight and feeble as she was. Before her my fearful heart felt naked. I believed she knew I was a coward, and would neither stand up for myself nor run away. She had a quiet but unshakeable air of omniscience. I fully believed she knew all the things one can learn on this earth. Matron's sister was a warm and gentle person who lived entirely in the shadow of her vigorous and successful sibling in her own remote world, impractical and inarticulate. The father was hot-tempered, a rough, rude man of whom I was afraid. After drinking, he became red-faced and surly. I saw in him an enemy blocking my path to the affections of all the women.

I had to remain in Perth for the physiotherapy and I began to live with the family. The nurses also lived in this house and a large front room was filled with their beds. Day and night I was consumed with my desire to see a woman's body. I expected the nurses to appease my appetite, but they seemed to have no inclination to undress, even before one another. I began to believe I was in love with every young girl I met. I loved the matron as a mother upon whom I depended, but I was in love with her young sister, though she was several years older than I. Paralysed by my shyness, I could never realise my ambition of a closer relationship than that of a strange guest, or dare to intimate my longing for love. Tormented by my thirst to see a woman's beauty, I asked if I could come into the bathroom while she was having a bath, on the pretext of having a wash. In her goodness, she allowed me, and the sight of her naked back filled me with joy.

My bed was on an open verandah beside the nurses' room. At night I crossed the road to Kings Park, and, hiding in the bush, encouraged by its silence, I sang. I had become infatuated by great singers, and aspired to join them. Shivering with cold and fear of being detected, I would sing wordless notes as loudly as I could, listening to my own voice for signs of greatness. The urge to sing was irresistible.

I began to read medical books. The orderliness and inevitability of the sequence of events in the preparation for an operation, at least as they were expounded by matron in an almost trance-like manner, greatly appealed to me. The means were so simple — a little steaming rectangular box, a handful of instruments, a cupboard full of linen — and the events so profound: life or death. The surgeon too, in whose hands lay all these workings of fate, was so retiring, disclaiming all honour and worship. This seemed to me how people should be. That I remained a domestic all my life perhaps is because this is the milieu in which I can best relive forgotten memories of my mother.

I used to go into the operating theatre and sterilising room when they were not being used, and gaze on the silvery, precise adjuncts to the awful art of medicine. A large room had been converted into the theatre, and was filled with the sun-like presence of the huge light over the slender operating table. Once I saw a cyst as large as a football lying in an enamel dish. Matron informed me nonchalantly that it had just been taken out of someone. I could not believe something so large could be inside a living person. Apparently the person still lived.

Matron knew many affluent and important people in the city, some of whom had been her patients. Such a one was a well-known barrister whom she persuaded to give me the opportunity of becoming a law clerk. My career began with running messages and between times sitting idly on a chair opposite the telephonist. She was a young girl with the deportment of a lady, luxuriously attired, often in a memorable deep brown dress that was too old for her. Of course, I fell in love with her in that beautiful brown dress. She must have guessed my lustful purpose, for her ill-disguised disdain showed me I was so far below her as to be untouchable.

After work I went to night school and learnt to balance accounts. Matron saw that I did my homework. I was wholly out of my element in both office and school. I swallowed the paralysing contradiction I was living every morning as I walked down the stone corridor of the high building to the glass doors of the hateful office where I assumed politeness and a subordinate position to everyone. The contradiction between my circumstances and my desire for freedom from subordination haunted me.

Some feeling was returning to my fingers, and I was encouraged to make plans for my future. Matron told me my doctor might put me through medicine, for she knew my curiosity on medical matters. I had been very affected by the death of a young girl in the hospital. A scratch had become infected when she was swimming in the river and she had died of septicaemia. As a special favour, matron allowed me to see the dead girl. She lay on a bed, her face like a marble carving. I was committed to the goal of becoming a doctor.

My doctor invited me to her luxurious home set in a tropical garden and as I sat there I realised the gulf that lay between my magnanimous benefactor and my stolid oppressed self. She was a woman of vision and would have given a higher education to every labouring man. I think she wanted to put me through medical school, but perhaps she could see I was too far behind, there would be too much education to catch up with. She didn't say anything direct, nor did I, and nothing came of it. But I thought she was a great woman. In her eyes lay the diagnosis and cure of the malady of our species. The cure was knowledge her whole energetic manner and angular frame seemed to say.

With my brown suitcase heavy with a double-breasted blue suit, I went back to Fairbridge Farm for a couple of days before I was assigned to a new job.

9

A Working Life

I was sent to work in the drought inured wheatbelt east of Perth, where the land is flat, the tree-lined horizon far away, and the earth often bare in spite of the rich chocolate soil. The grey rails taper away into obscure distance where, long before it is seen, the slowly approaching train is heralded by a muffled whistle. Finally, a plume of white smoke moves over the tops of the trees, and the train comes to a halt beside a rectangular board with a name on it, the only signal that here is a station. The road is as level as a table and wide as a city street, but empty, the far-flung sky an immense cup of space.

My duties were to milk a few cows, clean the stables where manure had been collecting for years in layers like ancient cultures, and to feed the sheep, which were invisible in the mulga of distant paddocks. I was assisted by an old horse and cart. Together we would take sacks of chaff and oats out to the sheep. I sat behind the leisurely treading horse as he sought his well-known way over ploughed land and through pathless expanses of dwarfed bush and low trees. The gums' glossy, widely spaced leaves, peeling, golden bark, and bare yellow limbs spread a golden light through the peaceful bush, where the only sound was the cart's wheel crushing the sand.

The ground was bare and the bushes all shorn as high as a sheep could reach. I emptied the sacks into the bins. There were always a few waiting sheep looking on philosophically. Parrots dispersed like coloured lightning. Here and there in the bush, without any predictability, were large circular shallow depressions, covered with a rime of salt, suggesting a more primitive earth. I was missing matron, and the land mirrored my desolation. Nevertheless, I was surprised and astonished by the new beauties of this unimaginable country, captivated by the light-filled air, pure colours and fluid sounds; the light on the bare skin of the gums which had shed their bark, the rich browns of the shed bark, trailing down like skirts and the emphatic, almost articulate, speech of the parrots. Even the grey of the sheep's wool seemed to jump out into one's eyes. The all-embracing silence admonished my perverse, rebellious thoughts. Although I was unused to writing letters and never received them, I debated with myself while wandering through the bush what I would say in a letter to matron. In spite of her dominating ways, I loved her. When she was dangerously ill with pneumonia, I had prayed for her, contemplating her death as a catastrophic loss, although I had long thought of myself as an atheist.

With the horse and cart I collected dead roots unearthed by the plough, trailing behind the sleep-walking horse for miles over acres and acres of soil, which lay patiently waiting for rain. I would envy the team of horses working in the distance, crawling over the earth around newly painted soil. Jim's small figure would be perched on the high seat over the plough, oblivious to everything except the ruling of his furrows. When Jim, a youth a year or two older than I, but already an experienced teamster, began sowing wheat, I would carry fertiliser out to the drill, the cart rocking on the tilled earth. The dead weight of the coarse bags of superphosphate threatened to demolish me as I staggered with them the few yards to the cart, loading and unloading. I was determined to claim this mark of a man, to transport two hundred pounds on my back, although I knew the weight was too much for me. I envied the ease with which Jim carried the bags in his arms, like nursing a baby.

Returning the horses at night, Jim walked home behind them with long reins in the dusk, his whole figure bent with fatigue and covered with dust. Night had already fallen behind him. I unharnessed and fed the team in the stables, emptying the chaff and oats under their snuffling noses. Later, with a hurricane lamp, I would go back to the stables, now pitch dark and sonorous with the rhythmical munching of the horses, and push my way past their heavy sides to see if their mangers needed replenishing. The cold night was accompanied by masses of stars, their number beyond computation and their distance unmeasurable. I was certain the universe could have no end or beginning. Time seemed to be a bit of human chicanery.

I had the task of cleaning out the stables. Manure was thickly impacted over the whole yard and around the stalls it was up to a foot thick. I was determined to expose the earth everywhere and start with a clean slate, but this took so long that I incurred the morose, silent criticism of the boss. I had to admit defeat as the nightly trodden manure in the stalls implacably resisted my long-handled shovel. The old horse took out load after load of it, but I never came to the end of it, and I was taken off the job.

Jim and I lived in a small wooden hut facing the eastern horizon. The roof overhung a bench with an enamel bowl for washing. My bed was under a window, from which I could see the first light of dawn. Jim got up in what seemed the depth of night, so freshly were the stars still blazing, but soon after he had left and I forced myself to stir, the pale tint of dawn would sweep the horizon and the stars begin to lose their fire. Jim groomed and fed his horses. Immediately after breakfast, which we ate at the table covered with oilcloth in the large neat kitchen of the boss's house, he would be seen disappearing into the sun behind his six possessed horses, a battered felt hat over his shining hair and lean tanned face. I emulated all he did, his strength, his familiarity with the land, with animals and with men, especially our formidable boss, of whose ponderous, moody frame I was perpetually apprehensive.

Sunday was the only day we had to ourselves, apart from attending to the animals. We washed our working clothes and gave ourselves a bath in a galvanised iron tub on the middle of the floor in the hut. Midday dinner on Sundays was the best meal of the week, for which we used to spruce ourselves up, spending a few minutes in front of the mirror, feeding our vanity. One fine Sunday, dressed in our best clothes, Jim and I went to see a friend of his. Jim gripped the steering wheel of his battered old utility with obvious satisfaction, and, transmuted by his suit, surveyed the country like its owner.

Jim's friend had borrowed money from the rural bank to establish himself and his family on a property. He was in financial difficulties and had sent his wife and children away while he lived on the pittance the bank allowed for food each week. It appropriated all he marketed from the farm as payment for the land. His appearance reflected his position. Alone in the empty, untidy house, he was a pitiful figure, emaciated and despondent, his lean face preoccupied with stifled wrongs. He had little machinery and this had broken down. A heavy rusty plough was collapsed just outside the door. We looked like two ignorant swells in our best suits and plastered hair, visiting this courageous, lonely man dressed in crumpled shirt and trousers. His hair was uncombed and his feet bare. He took no umbrage at our appearance and immediately set about getting us something to eat and drink, in a movingly clumsy way.

Jim and he were soon thrashing out his farm problems, Jim as passionate as though they were his own, while, in abashed innocence, I sat and listened. Jim insisted he could restore the broken plough, which we went out to inspect. It seemed to be irrevocably seized with rust, but Jim asserted he would return and repair it. I could see little cultivated ground and the walls of the bush rose inauspiciously close to the house. In spite of one's prayers for a reversal in the relentless fate of this man, one could apprehend only inevitable defeat for him. We departed, disturbed in the bland silence and inimical emptiness of the bush.

I had become a devotee of work morality, almost a religion of work. It was not preached to me. I learnt it by example from the farm workers. As I had been committed to remove every speck of manure from the stable yard, so my religion necessitated my extracting every shred of couch from the dry garden when I was told to tidy it up because the boss's new wife was coming. It was as though I was collecting my works against an imminent judgement day. I enjoyed work not for its own sake, as convention required, but for the remission of sin, and therefore, its liberation from guilt and pain. The guilt-laden soul finds relief in labour, digging its own grave and priding itself on the good job it has done.

Red earth, blue sky and sun, all drawn so artlessly in the fierce light. Yet in the garden, like a memory of a long forgotten past, grew snapdragons on a meagre ration of water. An ebullient, green peppercorn tree leant over the fence wire outside the kitchen. I crushed its thin juicy leaves and tiny orange berries, rolling the pip in my sticky fingers, sniffing its magic aroma. For days I struggled with the couch, inextricably lodged in the rock-like soil.

One day an unexpected lone figure approached, bent beneath a burden. He asked me for some hot water, and when I went to the kitchen to tell the housekeeper, she immediately understood and asked if the man required tea, sugar, or meat. All of these things were doled out into small packages and passed to the man, who stowed them away happily in his worn, stained sugar bag. Then he continued down the road. I followed him as far as I could and longed to leave my oppressive toil and meet him on the brow of the distant hill for a talk. But I dared not leave my post.

I sat in the hut reading at night, the lamp-glass swelling with yellow light illuminating the packed type in the Oxford book of poems. The deathly silence of the earth outside. Bent over the frail page, afraid of angering Jim with the light, Byron or Shelley, line after line, insisting on the light a little longer. Stiffened with cold, convinced by fatigue, extinguishing with a puff the oily flame, and penetrating the cold rough blankets. Repeating to myself the music of my own language in poetry, the music I had heard as a child. I shrank from the bad language pervasive in the bush. I searched for perfect poems, little interested in their meaning. As one of the oppressed millions, I could not evade the import of the meaning in Shelley.

I was never comfortable with any bosses but this one in particular disconcerted me. He remained obstinately taciturn, self-absorbed, glum. He made no attempt to become acquainted with me and I was too afraid of him to try to broach his reserve. Only once did I work with him, and this was the only time I saw him doing anything on his farm, he left everything to Jim. He wanted me to assist him on horseback, searching for a few lost cattle in forest adjacent to the homestead. I had never learnt how to ride a horse. Jim saddled a horse for me and encouraged me. The horse was remarkably quiet and seemed resigned to a walk. I desperately hoped we would not find any cattle, anticipating the choking embarrassment of falling off my horse if he had to go any faster.

I worked together with that man the whole afternoon without his once acknowledging my existence, without a word from him to me. He seemed buried in thoughts that would never see the light of day. His heavy face was foreboding. It was beautiful in the forest but we were two inarticulate human beings. The boss was about to be married and bring his wife home. Perhaps the years of silence and isolation in which he had lived alone with an elderly housekeeper in an empty house had stilled his tongue.

At last I was leaving the wheatbelt. I had been there a year. I lodged in a lonely guest house by the railway line for the night and ate a homely breakfast. Then I left the brief good fortune of a room of my own, with its varnished furniture and white sheets, and went to stand by the railway line with my one large case, warmed by the low sun, and overwhelmed by the infinite space of golden light.

I went back to Fairbridge Farm for a few days before being sent out to work again, and I wandered over some of the old haunts. I loitered past the Colonel's munificent garden. Its bountiful grape vines gave every cottage massive bunches of grapes every year, brought home exultingly in wide tin pans and shared out with scrupulous justice by the cottage mother. The Colonel was indeed a benevolent tyrant, and was loved by us all in those hot summer days. I walked down to the river, over the ancient bridge and along the narrow path, graven by countless naked feet, to the broad pool in the bend of the river. There, I had once thought I was going to be drowned by an older boy holding my head under the water. I climbed again the first range where colossal granite boulders were strewn over the steep hillside. To man, all was in confusion, chaotic, but one knew that here, there was a natural order.

I was sent this time to a farm in Bridgetown. The original weatherboard homestead had been abandoned by the farmer who now lived in a luxurious brick house, and here I bunked with the other labourers. The buildings were dilapidated and scourged a dirty grey by sun and rain. Only the two rooms of a married man, Hughie, had any furniture or features of comfort, his bedroom incongruously displaying white lace curtains. His other room was a large kitchen, with a homely wood stove and a large deal table, but when he invited us single men in for a cup of tea, there were never enough chairs. Hughie was the manager of the shorthorn stud cattle. We seldom saw his small, pretty wife who was ailing with an obscure malady, and she shortly had to leave for the city with her two young children. I think Hughie was heartbroken. I remember her pale oval face, beautiful with an inner life of thought and understanding, haunted with the threat of disappearing. Her large eyes dwelt on you, looking for more than was there. Her two small children clung to her. Hughie was small too, a wiry bushman and a leader. I was to help him with the stud cattle. It was a revelation to see the calmness with which he did everything. He would step into the pen where the enormous shorthorn bull stood with lowered head, seemingly bent on total annihilation, and with deliberate steps Hughie would walk up to him. Placing one hand on his shoulder, he would begin brushing his coat. Hughie never hurried any animal. I never saw him impatient with anybody, and what most astonished me was the way he persuaded the boss to agree with him. The boss was a proud, autocratic man, but he deferred, like a child, to Hughie's natural authority.

The large room where the single men lived was bare of furniture, except for the narrow beds against the walls. In the middle of the bare floor stood the blackened hurricane lamp, the only source of light. At night, I would leave it alight as long as I dared, straining to read in the gloom, at the risk of annoying the two other labourers who had to get up at four to go to the big milking shed. They seldom complained. They were so tired with the relentless labour of milking the herd of nearly two hundred cows that they slept like logs and in the early morning, like a distant memory, their moving about faintly impinged on my consciousness.

In the morning I would take a pail of milk up to Louise, the cook, in the boss's kitchen. She prepared our meals, too extravagantly to the boss's irritation, for she was a large generous woman, sympathetic to the workers. We sat at a long table, neatly set on the verandah outside the kitchen, from where we could see the warming figure of Louise moving commandingly within. It was a pleasure for us lonely single men to watch a good-looking woman working on our behalf.

Hughie befriended me and made me feel for the first time that I might be an independent individual, something rare in the strict hierarchy of the bush, where experience imposes an implicit system of rank upon men. Although Hughie had a lifetime of experience and I had practically none, he treated me as an equal. I was disconcerted by the deference he seemed to pay me for my useless prattle of city education, which perhaps reflected his profound hope for the education of his two children. The future for a working man's children was bleak. I felt Hughie afforded some protection for me. Later, my obstinate desire for independence asserted itself and he made me feel that I had wounded his faith in me in a way he would not forget. I could do nothing about it. I had to have my way. So blind is man. To manipulate a few cold material things in his own egotistical way, he will ignore the warm hands of friends and lovers, to his lifelong impoverishment and shame.

High, stony and densely forested hills lay close beside the steep gravel road that ran up to the new house. On the other side, unbroken fillies were kept in a cleared treeless paddock, to be trained as riding horses for the boss's teenage daughter and her friends. In common with daughters of other landed men, the boss's daughter imitated her father, rode like him with her back and head erect, and maintained his ascetic expression. Her pale, dry beauty suited the enslaving romanticism of the time. I loved her for what I admired and feared in her father: his tall, thin, spartan figure, pale countenance and resolute, impenetrable expression. She laughed at me, in company with her school friend, a dumpy, cheerful girl, whose spontaneity and amiable brown eyes struck a deeper chord in my exiled heart. I dared not show, by any omission of devoted glances, that I was disloyal to the boss, her father. But secretly, to myself I avowed that her friend and I were the real lovers, who one day would confirm it in each other's eyes and words, and would travel through the rest of our transformed lives together.

Once a year, Hughie prepared the pampered cattle for the Bridgetown Show. He lathered the soap into their rough coats and brushed and combed them for weeks prior to the event. Even their horns were polished. At the showground they blazoned their owner's name to the congregation, parading the oval with measured tread in their yearly tribute of gold, blue and white ribbon, Hughie leading the champion bull by the nose. I was not considered experienced enough to go in the show ring, so I haunted the pens, marvelling at the size of the pigs. It was taken for granted that our animals would get all the prizes.

Two brothers owned this farm, and they were so unlike as to excite speculation on the sources of human character. My boss's brother ran the big dairy farm, and struck me as an ingenuous, pagan god, while my boss was an arrogant, civilised dandy. His self-righteous, habitually rebuking expression, his expensive working clothes, reinforced all the guilt in my soul. The benign, wonder-captured expression of his brother recalled one to archaic dreams of freedom. His movements were loose and surrendering, his clothes ragged and ill-fitting. It was as though he were there merely as a duty to the gods, and his real place was among the blessed spirits of the undisturbed forests of remote mountains. Though I felt an affinity with him, it did not dissolve my natural dread of anyone in authority. My hatred for his brother was more real than this incipient love for him, for I had to obey my boss's commands in fact, not in fancy.

Every word my boss uttered was as if issued from a god, telling his creatures to bow down. Even though a creature may be stretching to pick high apples, inwardly, he is bowing down with his hatred before his master. Soon, the creature's own creative divinity asserts itself, and accepts joyfully the work the earth affords. This is not easy, however, when the servant and master have to work closely together.

I bought a bicycle in Bridgetown. On Sundays I would ride for miles on the rough, steep, gum-lined roads, winding along narrow ridges so that one could contemplate far below, as far as one could see, patterns of a rich cultivated valley growing wider and more obscure in the distance. An orchard with avenues of ancient trees burdened with swollen fruit, golden plums or crimson peaches, hanging over the old, gaping fence, proffered refreshment after a gruelling climb. I was fleeing from haunting dreams of black-clad figures with faces of stone announcing condign sentence, fleeing from loneliness for life, fleeing from self-cringing, from cruel hands, burning fingers, stinging back; fleeing to find a woman to assuage my devastation. The woman proved to be the earth: her orchard-embellished hills, her pure azure skies, her flocks of sheep, her herds of cows in spacious paddocks. I lost myself in the beauty of the country, the tree-lined river.

I was still so English as to wear the navy blue suit and tie that matron had bought me in Perth for the office, and sweat poured off me as I pedalled the twenty miles or so to Greenbushes for a fete. A row of astonishingly tall pine trees lined the sports field of a small weatherboard school. A few grown-ups trod aimlessly about on the unfamiliar school playground, or stood in small solid groups, conversing seriously. The children's races were being prepared. And I saw her, the amazon-like girl with the ancient face who seemed always to be at such gatherings like a spirit of time, and whom I should always love and fear. She was the spirit of dance and music, unrecognised in this country of strength and rivalry. But everyone sensed her importance.

In my city suit and nursing my city self-image, I was an alien: I was among better people than myself. I could not speak their language and I could not move like them with their strength and assurance. How debonair the countrymen were! I did not have their horizon glance. I was still tied up in the roads of London. There were two handsome brothers who were well-known in the district. They were sunny, benevolent, and willing to help everyone. They seemed inseparable. I longed for their friendship but I was unable to overcome my awe of them. The elder brother had marvellous strength and that day I saw him win the sheaf-tossing competition. The last race of the day was an egg-and-spoon race for the adults. Of course I did not enter it. I joined the crowd to watch the buck-jumping. No one could stay on the steers, which were unfairly excited by a rope between their back legs. What enormous energy was unlocked, fruitlessly, in that tiny railed yard. In imagination, I saw myself riding one of the steers victoriously.

The physically powerful are often vulnerable in the field of emotions. A young sleeper cutter on the farm, Len, who had once worked for the two brothers, had become engaged to Louise, the cook. He was a lovable fellow of bear-like frame and proverbial strength, but of extreme sensitivity of feeling, an incipient imbalance and derangement with which I felt some affinity. For a long time he used to visit her at night, hanging about the house in the dark, before she accepted him. Suddenly he became possessed by ridiculous suspicions that Frank, a handsome farm labourer who lived with us, was pursuing her. One evening he came determined to fight, believing his rival to be with Louise, and only Hughie's words stopped him from going up to the boss's house. It was possible he would have killed Louise, of whom we were all fond. It was moving to see how Hughie protected Len from himself. Hughie asked me to go up and see if Louise would see Len. With some trepidation I did so. She answered my call but would not see him. It was obvious no one was there with her. The two eventually got married.

I continued on in my wall-less prison of labour and servitude, to serve out my years until I would reach twenty-one. It is the tedium of the oppressive regime that eventually makes man throw it off. I pushed countless deep boxes of apples into the yawning back of the cart, and walked beside it countless times, with the long leather reins attached to the horse, as in a ritual, among the trees to the packing shed.

I asked Fairbridge to find me another place, and I left the brothers' farm, where I was one of many labourers, for a small family farm where dairying and orchard work were my main occupations. Here I could read after work, before setting the alarm clock and getting into my unmade bed. The glass of the oil lamp would become coated with soot, as I strained my eyes until the last glimmer of light was gone. I found some little Nelson's classics of Scott's novels left in the room, and got carried away far into the night by their adventures.

I was used, now, to stumbling through the soaking clover in the misty mornings, gathering the somnolent cows into a chain of acquiescent animals winding its way down to the milking shed where I would milk them, determined to get faster at this indispensable duty. Speed was the first goal on the land. Those who were fast were admired and courted by the ever hungry farmer. I improved my skill with the separator, watching the thick pale yellow cream draw out of the frothy milk, and dismantling and reassembling the intricate machine with ever increasing confidence.

The boss was leaving everything to me and I gained confidence in managing the farm and delight in being independent. I was now nineteen. As the apple blossom turned to little green apples, I bent under the wide spreading branches to dig painfully around their dark trunks.

The boss and his wife were a quiet couple who liked to stay in their little wooden cottage and garden. This suited me for, as must be clear by now, I hated taking orders. It was with dismay that I saw I was not to be relied on to pack apples. Strangers with professional eyes to judge were brought in for it and I became again the farm labourer, not the manager, and piled up the heavy packing boxes down the centre of the packing shed. I was given the responsibility of making apple boxes out of the red slices of jarrah, learning self-approvingly to knock home the flat-headed nails with just two flourishing taps. The hot hours passed, making up cases, bringing home loads of apples in the horse and cart, squeezing more and more replete cases into the dark packing shed.

How ashamed I was of being regarded as a labourer. Farm labourer seemed to me to be the most obnoxious appellation upon earth, as though such a person had only muscles and no brain. The new work I was doing was a constant challenge to me both physically and mentally, for instance, cutting silage from the compressed tangled block of green clover and grass I found almost beyond my strength. A broad bladed curved knife, as long as a sabre or cutlass was used to carve out a sufficient portion for the herd of twenty cows.

I felt the family liked me and there was some understanding between us, but I was nevertheless moved on, for this little group of cockies on the Bridgetown–Manjimup Road seemed to be moving me from one to another. I think I had been recommended as a good worker, which pleased my vanity no end.

My new young boss left me to myself as well, with a herd of about twenty cows to milk, night and morning, by hand of course. I enjoyed accomplishing this, filling the cream can with cream, and taking up the old lady half a bucket of fresh milk. This little farm of one hundred acres was on the edge of untouched bush, which I often explored on Sundays. The silence, harmony and effortless freshness of the bush impressed me indelibly. I felt more at home in it than I had ever felt anywhere. And yet, across the boundary fence, on the young man's new property, I prided myself on rolling the fallen trees into heaps and burning them. After tea, I would go out into the fire-strewn night and pull the dying logs together, until eventually they were a grey and orange quilt of ash on the bare ground. I loved using the simple tools, the crowbar and hook, to such unexpected effect, and loved the sense of power over such massive, seemingly invincible weights, and the scourging use of fire. I was left entirely to my own devices and felt my sense of independence growing.

Then I was sent to work for an elderly couple a few miles south. They were never quite well and it was obvious the work of a farm was getting too much for the husband. They both treated me kindly, were curious about me, and seemed to understand my loneliness.

Not far from their house was a wooden hut in which I lived. There were two rooms, one full of old magazines and books, the other, with the single window, containing a bed and table. Here, among a host of scurrilous magazines, I found my first great book, *Pride and Prejudice*, which I read very slowly, with astonishment and delight. I discovered for the first time the beauty of my language. The book exercised a fascination over me for a long time. I suppose my new employers were genteel people, like those in the book.

There was a lot of half-cleared land on this farm, and I thought it my mission to finish clearing it. So whenever possible I set about my new vocation of pulling up scattered grey logs and setting them alight. The boss and his wife would bring afternoon tea to me, walking through the trees like young lovers. I was very self-conscious being looked after by such a beautiful pair. The tall, thin figure of my master haunted the milking shed with his solicitude for his shiny new milking machine.

These were a novelty and made milking much easier, but they were still unreliable and the boss was painfully anxious about it. I was nervous of its bits and pieces and was sure it would not equal the thoroughness with which my own hands would have done the milking. But it was impossible not to relinquish the exhausting routine of hand-milking for the easy approximation to nature of the machine.

An unforgettable character lived on this farm in an especially privileged position. The boss seemed to be repaying him for some past favour. He was a giant of over seven feet and lived by himself in a cottage in the middle of the orchard. Every day he went sleeper-cutting down the line. He was a student of meteorology and kept daily records of the wind velocity and direction, the rainfall, the barometric pressure, and no doubt, of other more recondite features of the climate. Occasionally he would help us on the farm and the boss deferred to him in all farm matters as to a professional agronomist. He was an educated man, always obliging and kind, and I could not fathom the mystery of his presence there, alone in the middle of the orchard. He was the first person with whom I could raise philosophical questions, and he gave me an intimation that the world might be understood and gone along with, instead of being fought and subjected. I wanted to be his friend but he was remote and reserved, and I was afraid of his enormous size and strength.

Across the road was the local hall where every now and then there would be a dance. In spite of my torments of shyness, I took the lure of love's promise — the rows of handsome girls seated on each side of the hall. I dressed myself in my navy blue suit, despite the hot night and the stifling hall. Romantic adventure occupied my mind, yet I remained imprisoned in my solitary cell no less than when I was still a child locked in my room. Spilling over into the night were the immaculately dressed and groomed young men, smelling of brilliantine and soap. In the porch and inside the entrance to the dance floor they were packed, so that one could hardly move. Their bright eyes travelled unceasingly among the girls, their red faces burst out of their tight collars and their flattened hair shone.

Enviously I watched the closely pressed couples gliding by, petrified by strangled desire. The girl I thought I loved was always quickly snatched up. Without enthusiasm, I would approach a girl who had been overlooked, and then the painful revelation that I could not dance would overcome me. Back among the boys, I was crushed by thoughts of my cowardice, for I could not bring myself to lead the rush onto the floor to secure the girl I loved. As the night wore on and the press of boys grew less, I found myself dancing, in agonies of embarrassment as I groped in vain for something to say, until I left my partner, inflamed with self-hatred and debased with shame. I made the bitter walk home under the meaningless stars, tossed by proliferating regrets. In the indifferent walls of an alien room, erasing and re-drawing all the scenes of love over and over again, I fell asleep.

I took many long walks into the bush by myself and once or twice got lost. This always seized me with panic, but some sense seemed to reassert itself so that I found my way home. One could be away all day and never see a soul or any evidence of the hand of man. Everything was pristine, logical, material, and an affirmation of destiny.

Inexorably, one's life disappears before one's inner gaze. How little I can recall of even a few years ago. My next job was on an orange orchard belonging to a young man and his mother. The son was away most of the time so I managed the farm, though I was only paid as a labourer. The incessant, monotonous toil was becoming increasingly oppressive, especially when I read Byron's poems, which proselytised romantic ideas of individual freedom. I would retire at night to light my ever-sooty hurricane lamp, and begin studying the love poems of Byron. I found an Oxford edition of his collected poems when I bicycled one day the fifty odd miles to Bunbury. Having furnished my bicycle with a lamp and generator I could now ride home in the dark, painstakingly weaving my way through pot holes and corrugations in the gravel road. I was getting faster and faster on the bicycle and secretly fostered ambitions to be a racing cyclist, which was very popular then among young men.

The monotony of farm work continued against a background of rumours of war. One of my tedious duties was to see that every tree got a large earthen cup of water, by means of hastily dug drains. I struggled to extract a little milk from four or five starving cows, who seemed as reluctant as I to start the dismal day. I went through the pretence of cleaning the old shed, which was beyond cleaning. I saw advertisements for the militia in the Perth papers, and eventually I sent in an application. After milking, I would go to the house with my abject half-bucket of milk and the old lady would give me my breakfast in the kitchen. She was a kindly person yet seemed to disapprove of her son's employing me, which strengthened my ambition to leave. After breakfast, I would go to work in the orchard, sometimes harnessing two magnificent bay mares for the purpose of ploughing. The first time was torture to both man and beast, for the trees had grown so close together neither I nor the horses could see where we were going. I fell into a frenzy and confess I punched the horses mercilessly on their soft noses trying to bend them to my will. This was the first time I had done any ploughing, and although it was so painful in the orchard, I enjoyed the open paddock where I could dance along on the freshly turned earth. It was a miracle, the way the plough dug, lifted up and turned over the continuous ribbon of earth. With the plough's handles jumping erratically in my hands, I felt I was growing up and becoming a real worker. I liked picking the oranges best. The fruit seemed to burgeon inexhaustibly amidst the infinity of smooth, dark green leaves. I was beginning to feel my isolation more and more. I heard no word from the militia.

I rode my bicycle as far as Busselton one day and went to have a look at the sea. The country seemed desolate and empty. The few people who were watching a football match in Busselton were firmly tied together in families. I rode back home, indigestible loneliness stuck in my throat.

Not far from the farm was the usual country hall, and I braved another dance. I saw boys stumbling about as clumsily as I did. The girls were radiantly beautiful, so I plucked up the courage this time to ask the girl of my choice. From her hesitation, I understood she belonged already to someone else, but she let me take her. The way she danced made it unnecessary for me to do anything. She carried me with her by some sort of natural grace and rhythm. Momentarily, I was dancing in spite of myself. I caught uneasily the hostile glances of her boyfriend, and he saw to it I had no chance of dancing with her again. But I could not take my eyes off her and she became the focus of my Byronic dreams. I tried writing poems myself. I sent one of them to my dancing partner, and the polite letter I got back made me realise love, or rather, the idea of love, like other ideas, is not necessarily mutual.

The last farm I was to work on was a huge property near Northam. Rolling denuded hills were piled one over another, contracting the bare horizon. A niggardly down of grass was rent by twisted gullies, riddled with rabbit holes. Great flocks of sheep drifted over the bulging hills, while distant paddocks were full of crowded wheat. The boss was a big man always on a horse from whose height he looked down on you like a czar. His son, a big boy at college, emulated his father and also went about on horseback. I was mortified by my subservience to him. The horse was then the insignia of absolute authority. We labourers all slept in a single weatherboard room among the farm sheds and sat around a big table in the kitchen of the boss's house for our meals. These were very meagre, and as we were given no bed clothes I was often very cold at night. Everything was on a big scale and I enjoyed meeting the neverending work with which I was confronted, at harvest and in the shearing shed particularly.

Although I was nineteen, and expecting to join the militia any day, I was still regarded as a boy by everyone. I would have liked to have got to know the shearers but they were studiously oblivious of my existence, and of everybody else's. They treated the all-powerful boss with thinly veiled contempt. They camped by themselves and got their own meals. They made everyone feel inferior to them with their preoccupation and strained faces. While working, they seemed possessed by a relentless demon that ruled them all day. Their only independent action was taking a long draught from the water bag hanging above them.

When shearing was over, I was proud to have the mowing of a paddock of lush clover to myself. I had two horses and a small flat machine whose knives were driven by the wheels. I was happy working alone in the empty paddock, watched only by the silent trees. This was my last job on the land. At last I got a reply from Perth and, in a week I packed up and left to join the militia.

10

War

We lay on boards on the earth, sacks of straw under us and grey blankets on top. There were four boards to each tent and they fitted together like four blocks. We slept, protected by the spread canvas whose odour pervaded the tent's narrow space.

The ambulance unit, all under canvas and commanded by a benevolent old doctor, was sequestered some miles from the city, surrounded by benign paddocks and slumbering bush, invaded here and there by reaches of the Swan River. Here I was, surrendering myself to my arch enemy, authority, something I knew to be the bane of all I was. Yet I was eager to co-operate with the seemingly congenial authority of the older corporals and sergeants, and to learn the novel art of erecting a tent. I smothered my loneliness and embarrassing muteness with work. Soon, we were marching in fours along the silent country roads to where the little ambulances stood in the shadows of the gum trees, and the large marquee was erected as a hospital.

At night I strained my eyes over *The Republic*, and other dialogues of Plato, while my companions stretched out on the floor and talked endlessly to one another. They did not disturb me, although their presence put me in a state of continuous self-consciousness. I was afraid to make an independent movement or sound lest I attract their attention. I feared they would judge me rude, and resort to ridicule or even blows. I feared ridicule most. I was ridiculous in my own eyes but could not escape the posture of which I was a victim. I cultivated the pose of a scholar as one that would secure me from exposure as the weakling and coward I had learnt I was. But Plato was teaching me I perhaps possessed other attributes: goodness, high-mindedness and stoicism, of which those around me knew nothing, and which I practised unconsciously.

Plato's style intimated to me ineffable beauties at large in the universe, which I could see but not reach. I was content to remain suspended between heaven and earth. A tall, fair youth of classical features befriended me and took me home when we had leave. His mother was a small, exceedingly kind woman with a broad open face who devoted herself to our happiness from the moment of our arrival. Like my friend, she was a devotee of a religion that embraced a vegetarian diet, which they both strictly obeyed. This in spite of the difficulties it brought my friend in camp. I would often see him dipping into a bag of dried fruit stowed in his trouser pocket.

His older sister was a preacher in their church, and I was captured by the illusion of gaining her love. She seemed the kind of high-minded person with whom I could travel through philosophical realms. But I was no nearer being able to articulate my feelings. I feared her scandalised rebuff and the end of her brother's love.

Under a benevolent commander, life in camp was very easy, but a younger man took over and imposed on us an oppressive regime of incessant drill. He forced me to carry my hatred of him concealed as I marched to and fro, whither he wished, on the small parade ground buried in the heart of the bush, my eyes and heart on the distant trees. Here was one little man with three or four hundred obedient to his will, yet within each apparent automaton there rankled rebellious hatred. With each tread of my heavy boots, I pressed hatred into the ground and my heart grew sick with a tyranny that had no end.

I rented an upstairs room in a dingy house, in a depressing row that faced the busy grimy street. But I was full of pride to have a residence of my own. The carpet on the steep narrow staircase was a novelty, if threadbare. The last time I had climbed carpeted stairs was in London. At the top was a landing with a gas ring, and doors to the two rooms. My room looked down onto repeated back yards. I had a bed, a table and a wardrobe. The front room was occupied by a young girl and boy no older than myself, who had just got married. I was surprised and intrigued that such a young girl should get married. She seemed but school age and behind her closed door I never ceased listening to her happy laughter and excited giggling. I did my best to imagine the scene behind the door — from the commotion, they always seemed to be chasing one another about the room.

I applied to join the air force. The tall handsome officers in the recruiting centre seemed to want my devotion and went out of their way to make my enrolment possible, in spite of my inadequate education. They treated me like a gentleman. I walked into the city for lessons in mathematics, then took work home, struggling for hours, at the little table beneath the mantelpiece in my room. I had no radical understanding. I learnt by rote, memorising the arbitrary theorems with difficulty, but after six months I passed the examination, dreaming I might take my place as a member of the establishment. The gods to whom I looked contritely upwards seemed to accept me as one of them, much to my astonishment.

All the while, I was demented by a passion for an ideal woman I could never grasp but whom I saw in every girl I passed. I wandered alone in King's Park on Sundays. Occasionally, there were dances in the Town Hall, where I would spend an excruciating evening, the desire for love confounded by my shyness and ineptitude. The girls were polite and handsome, very strong in character and physique. I was afraid of their potential hatred, of public rejection. Guilty of prurient desires I stood defenceless. I brooded with regret over the girls I should have spoken to, recalling all their attractions and suggestions of friendliness, hating the polished floor and the crush of people that thwarted my success.

In the air force, among rich men's sons — the sons of landowners who had enslaved me since coming to Australia — I began that life-long contradiction between my past as a labourer and my masquerade as an educated man. The trouble was, the rich men's sons of Australia, who had been to good schools and to universities, did not pride themselves on their mental attributes, but on their physical ones. In these I remained patently inferior. I began to see myself as an imposter, intruding into a preserve from which I might suddenly be ejected ignominiously, and retreated into my self-consciousness as a scholar of poets and philosophers, recalling my faithful volumes of Plato, Montaigne, and Shakespeare, whose company awaited me as soon as I could be alone.

At Pearce Air Force station we were quartered in long weatherboard huts, our iron beds ranged side by side, with no recognition of the need for privacy and solitude. I found one friend here, a country boy like myself, with whom I could present a united front. He had a round face with red cheeks and friendly laughing eyes. We each found ourselves adrift in a hostile sea of conceit and pride. And drill. Perhaps war is nothing but the repetition of immemorial forms. The young cannot resist the ritual. Meaning crumbles before the madness of preordained universal movements. Down the streets of Perth we would march, three or four hundred replicas of the drill sergeant.

Selected to be trained as an observer, I joined a group that was sent to the observers' training school in Mt Gambier. I had left my chubby-faced friend behind. He was going to become a fighter pilot. We travelled across the desert by train, cooped up in small compartments. The intimate proximity of my companions disturbed me, for I still could never think of anything to talk about and would be agonisingly oppressed by any period of silence that settled between us.

A sort of flat inhumanity struck me like a blast of cold air as soon as we arrived at the Mt Gambier Air Force station. The friendliness of the West was gone and in its place a harsh impersonality reigned. An ominous emptiness and silence dwelt like a suffocating atmosphere over everything. The whole country was brooding under intense heat, but the desolating atmosphere of the base may have emanated from its commander, a forbidding, morose, and paternalistic figure; a gaunt, ascetic, Englishman.

We were quartered in huts. I kept a couple of books under my mattress. I was now falling under the influence of Schopenhauer, won by his beautiful style and irrefutable arguments for the supremacy of the individual conscience. I still wanted to live my private life and painfully felt the whirlpool of young men around me. They were taller, stronger, happy and spontaneous. I was inordinately nervous in the shuddering, roaring planes, confined with an omniscient instructor, the pilot, who really had no time to teach, and another trainee who was precocious and seemingly oblivious of my presence. I lost all presence of mind in the air and had no confidence in any of my blundering calculations. The pilot would look without moving a muscle at what I handed him and fly on. I could see I was superfluous. I was not afraid but totally confused. I needed to catch up what the more educated boys took for granted and there was no time for individual tuition.

The neat, toy like activity of man seen from the air was tantalising. How could we little creatures have done all that? As far as navigation went, everything I had studied in the stifling school room vanished, and I became a mindless piece of baggage, although filled with wonder and curiosity at all I saw through the small windows. I had no sense of direction, nor could I recognise landmarks. The pilots knew their way blindfold, so there seemed no urgency to provide them with directions. Anyway, it was impossible to concentrate on my drawing and calculations, owing to the noise and turbulence of the plane.

Little groups were formed and if you were not in one of those groups, no one spoke to you. It was the old school tie. Dressing up in my flying suit, I felt like a servant trying on his master's clothes. On the sports field I was totally at sea. In the afternoon study session I vainly tried to get accurate results with my obdurate instruments, then everyone would all tumble out onto the nearby paddock with a heavy medicine ball and a free-for-all would begin. I quickly learnt I was not made for that and remained in the classroom reading.

At weekends we had leave and, like a flock of birds, the four or five hundred trainees would disperse, many in civvies. They must have been taken home in cars, for none were to be seen in the dull abandoned town where I would go in an ancient bus, practically the only passenger. Tormented by my hunger for love and affection, I would wander through the lifeless main street in my suffocating uniform, for I had no civvies. Far from friendliness, there seemed to be a hostility towards airmen. I was led to understand by silences and stares that I was not welcome. They had a grudge against this English war. Finally, at one of the subdued dances held weekly in the town, a young girl befriended me and took me home. I had looked often at the houses nestling in the low hills. Now I was being taken to one. Although the girl and her mother were kind, setting the table especially for me with fragrant home-made cooking, her father regarded me with distrust, looking contemptuously on my uniform. He was no doubt afraid for the virtue of his daughter who was a very innocent and trusting girl. Indeed, I was ravenous for sexual experience. But the mother protected me from the father. She knew her daughter better, and the girl showed, unasked and unexpectedly, the affection, although not the sexual experience, I yearned for.

One weekend the heat drew me out to the volcanic lakes, which lay just outside the town. Boys were leaping about on the edge of the water, making me painfully conscious of my puny shoulders. My failure to develop explicit muscles particularly aggravated me, and was a source of habitual anxiety. The Brown Lake was a hundred yards across and no one was swimming in the centre. I was gripped by the idea of swimming across to the further shore, which was empty and untrammelled. But the water was cool and became colder as I got further from shore until cramp gripped one of my legs. I looked despairingly at the farther shore, and unhappily abandoned my determination to reach it. Slowly I crawled back, relieved I had excited no attention. But I had failed to accomplish this exploit, which I had set as a test of myself, and so I decided to challenge myself by climbing a narrow, high ridge to a lookout where there was a telescope. The path was only wide enough for one and from it, the sides fell precipitously, but by a great effort of will I managed it. I had always been terrified of heights, which exerted a morbid fascination over me, so that I could only just keep from throwing myself over.

11

Sydney

Reinforced by philosophy, which I took from its hiding place under the mattress before lights out, I began to be haunted by pacifist ideals. I was torn by the conflict of my thoughts, which during the night hours brooded over a surrender to pacifism, and in the day struggled with the strange and daunting ritual of preparing for war as well as shame at my backwardness in executing the plotting of courses.

   A laconic figure was one day introduced to us in the classroom as a visitor from the Royal Air Force. He spoke to us about bombing missions in Germany, and his explanation of how bombs were dropped on any light source when the military target could not be found, stuck in my thoughts and cemented my conviction that I must escape. I sent in a written resignation to the commander. I had to start living the pacifist dream. I was assigned to clerical duties in the office and shortly afterwards, discharged. In the office no one harassed me but I felt I was deserting my fellow men. I found my file and discovered I was branded as lacking moral fibre, which somehow corroborated all I had ever felt about myself, but had never known how to crystallise so concisely. But I also felt keenly the injustice of this publicly displayed verdict. Although I knew all too well my own cowardice, I felt I had done the only thing I could to abolish war. My superiors did not understand the love between men that the philosophers talked about. It was as though they preferred not to know themselves.

I reached Sydney in the middle of a heat wave. Water was severely rationed and the air stood in waves above the sticky black roads. I sought out the second-hand book shops; a little one in Castlereagh Street run by a kind-faced man who seemed omniscient among books, and Tyrells in George Street where I first found the books of Friedrich Nietzsche in their mysterious and beloved black covers. For several years, and over many miles, these recondite volumes would accompany me, sustaining my weak spirit against the indifference of men and the loneliness in my heart.

I now tried to start living as though the war did not exist. But I had only left a small cage for a larger one. After the long train journey from Mt Gambier, I walked blindly up Pitt Street where the broad unfurnished vestibule and wide stone steps of the People's Palace seemed to offer an invitation. I walked into the large foyer towards the tiny office, and was provided with a cell-like room with a low iron bed, a dressing table with a Bible, and the unexpected novelty of a wardrobe, an inscrutable luxury. Through the large sash window I looked down into a quarry-like square. The simple solution to the ideal of peace — being peaceful — seemed to have won a precarious victory.

My want of education began to irk me in the more

sophisticated world opening up before me, for I began to haunt the little theatres that were scattered temptingly around Sydney. Mrs Bryant of Bryant's Playhouse was very good to me, inviting me home and prompting me to study acting, but I could not even dream of it. Her tall student son was supercilious and her beautiful daughter, the embodiment of all my romantic dreams, unapproachable by so inarticulate and clumsy a worshipper as myself.

I liked the people of the New Theatre. They seemed sympathetic in my longing for something irrevocably lost. They were naturally friendly and concerned about the future of mankind. But they expected more of me than I was capable of giving. I could never act. No one seemed to realise how bottomlessly self-conscious I was. I used to leave the ramshackle theatre with the gulf widening in my heart, knowing, with painful awareness, my ineptness with the very people I imagined I loved. I sat alone watching rehearsals of *Le Tartuffe*, thrilled at the new freedom these people gave me to come and go as I pleased, to watch their world as much as I liked and at the modesty with which they did such surprising things. This was what I wanted my world to be like. They urged me to be one of them, but I could only sit and gape.

In the narrow corridors of the People's Palace I got to know two girls from Melbourne. They were close friends and their infectious good humour eased my shyness. I soon became besotted with passion and expectation. One of the girls was small and dark, her face elfish and indrawn. Such girls always seem to remind me of my mother. She yielded to my invitation to visit my small stony room, where we sat on the hard bed and talked about her life in a factory in Melbourne. She allowed my fumbling attempts to undress her but I was shocked by the darkness of her breasts. While I was struggling to suppress my sudden repugnance her friend knocked on the door. She seemed as upset as I was at the intrusion, but my frustration was not without some relief.

I began looking for work, determined to maintain my distance from the war. I was soon disillusioned. Upon going to a cigarette factory, the wily foreman with an ever ready smile said he would have to see my discharge certificate when I told him I had been in the air force. I realised this would be the routine, and as I had already destroyed my discharge certificate because of its offending allusion to my want of moral fibre, I was unlikely to get a job anywhere.

Every day I passed the recruiting depot in the middle of Martin Place, an innocuous looking booth, like a makeshift theatre. I was torn by irreconcilable instincts, love of mankind on the one hand, and my own survival on the other. It became more plain each day that I could not survive in my own solitary peace. Unable to explain my defection from the air force, I would not be given work, and my money was rapidly vanishing. With leaden steps I mounted the wooden dais of the recruiting depot and asked if I could join the medical corp of the army and be guaranteed the job of a stretcher bearer. I was assured I could. The army seemed far more obliging than the air force. I signed the required form and descended to the indifferent footpath with relief. I now had a little room in Kings Cross, where I was watched closely by a contemptuous protectress of the nation's morals. There I waited above the tin letter box, mentally flagellating myself for my treachery, but at the same time anxiously awaiting my call-up papers. My problem was one of desperate loneliness. I was totally without any connection with my fellow men, although surrounded by them. At length, I found the crucial letter in the mail box.

On the half-lit streets of Kings Cross she stood, looking deliberately away from me and from all men into the flashing lights of the traffic. Loneliness drove me to stand beside her, and under her breath she told me her prices. Less under a bush, more in her room. She was ill. My desire gave way to pity and she led me through a nearby door, up a flight of stone steps to her room with its curtainless window. We sat beside one another on the bed. She told me she had consumption and complained of the callous way in which the government treated incurable people like herself. She lived on quicksand, which might sink under her at any moment, and without a single hand stretched out to her in love or affection. I became as callous as the rest and left her, afraid to touch her for fear of contracting the dreadful disease, and oppressed by the ominous clinging smell in her room. Yet, I had often imagined myself dying a death of consumption. It was easy and quite conventional to die of the romantic idea of it, almost a qualifying suffering for the genius and artist of those times — sitting in the cafe before one's coffee, imagining one's body decomposing within, a look of sublime resignation on one's face.

I was the image of stone steps. Their texture and shape formulated the incommunicable self. I was the brown walls of implacable English justice and the grey unyielding footpath of the only way. The stone god of the city imposed his authority on my daydreams of freedom and love. The soaring arch of the bridge momentarily echoed my feelings. Over the side, the sheer drop into eternity. The shanty town of Sydney offered resounding hollow homes, and these I received as images of myself. The grey monsters of the ocean waited outside the Woolloomooloo pubs. My history grew out of simultaneously destructive and creative demons. I divulged my soul to no one. All the many faces of extermination followed me with the inevitable chastisement as an imposter, an intruder. I was worthy only of reprisals for sin. I was an Old Testament example, suffering the lord's disfavour, the sin of birth and severe retribution. I lived within the pages of a book, fastened by simple words that I gave my first passion. It was the book that incorporated me in man, although a man of whom the rest are ashamed. We are still a biblical herd, a congregation, still imprisoned in the word, because it is the creator of life. All books are only the Bible. The very matrix in which one lives is punitive and patriarchal. All other cultures have been translated into the Old Testament. The written language is itself immediately a religion. I should abjure the written language, but I love god-like words. In spite of the illusion that one can love everybody, I find that I have the ability to love only a specific form. The reality one pursues turns out again and again to be a deceptive likeness. I spent my first weeks in Sydney pursuing a vision of beauty that momentarily rested on the face of every girl I saw.

The showground's pavilions seemed built to enclose the whole population. My heart contracted in despair at this proof that I was sinking in the nameless mass. I wanted to flee, but fear of retribution stopped me, and anyway I knew I could not survive out of the army. Prison, the haven of many pacifists, did not occur to me. Naked to the waist, we filed dumb and passive before the doctors who examined us perfunctorily, and then moved us on to the quartermaster's minions. My uniform felt like a coarse, heavy bag. Blinkered under my hat, my boots were like lead casks that I had to deliberately raise and lower. This all added to my self-consciousness as I, waiting like a tin soldier at a stop, boarded the tram and found a seat under the amused stares of women and the contemptuous glances of men. Only by suppressing all my independence and yearning for freedom could I confront the single soldier at the gate and obsequiously show him my pass.

The Services' Club in Macleay Street had the facade of an exclusive hotel. Now I was in uniform I had the privilege of staying there, along with a continually milling crowd of other uniformed men, waited on by well-dressed girls. With dog-like devotion I tried to tell them with my eyes of my chronic loneliness but they seemed oblivious of my suffering.

I felt at home in Macleay Street. It revived memories of my early childhood in London. The well-dressed, confident people carried on normally in spite of the war. Nearby, were several small cosmopolitan cafes. One was on a promontory overlooking the pavement. The white lacework of the tables and the garden, raised like a stage above the road, eased my brooding over memories of London and its spacious gardens. After overcoming my trepidation before the heavy glass doors, I hastened through and out to a table at the far end of the garden, overlooking the street. The white wrought iron tabletop and chair were so heavy that, once seated, I felt anxious about extricating myself. I knew I should not really be here. I was breaking class taboos. In civilian clothes I would never have come in here. The waitress served me with coffee, her silence an eloquent rebuff. She — and the other members of the staff — knew I had come there to steal a girl, who would be sitting at one of the tables by herself, like a vase of flowers. But there were no girls sitting alone with their magical coffee. A fat man had a beautiful tall girl. His round stomach was like a melon, his face was full and smooth, and pronounced me guilty for coveting his money and girl. He slid between the tables and looked at no one, not even his girl. She hung after him with an irritated air, a tall dark shadow in chains.

At another cafe a little further down the wide exotic street two Frenchmen sat proclaiming freedom so loudly and learnedly that I realised I did not know how to speak or live. The owner of the cafe was in a dudgeon because the place was not paying. I could stay as long as I liked. The narrow walls of the cafe were like a tomb, and I could leave my body to it, and wander off into an incorporeal world. They would not throw me out when I might yet buy more.

I could not reconcile being in the army with my conscience. My heart contracted beneath the fetters, the prisoner-like uniform imbued me with self-hatred. I was an accomplice to the authority I hated and feared, an accessory to the crime of society against myself. I grovelled at the feet of every petty tyrant rather than risk rejection, and self-righteously congratulated myself on the performance of every loathsome duty. I presented my leave pass triumphantly to the detested corporal on the gate. I raised my arm obsequiously to the officers, while I sank into the ground with embarrassment for such self-abasement. I avoided people in authority and read books whenever I could.

The book on the table remains when the ideas have faded, the images are forgotten. Men want to deny their own weakness and cowardice, their desertion of themselves for the safety of the mob. They subscribe to the devastation of their personal lives in order to escape loneliness and exile.

The number, the uniform, again. The ignominy of obedience. I was everybody's tool again. We loitered on the station watching our kitbags and packs, waiting like animals to be entrained into the unknown. I looked shamefully at my uniform, like some monster skin I was forced to occupy. My misery in the army never left me.

Infantry training camp was held in a broad grassy valley near Cowra, resounding with the devastating noise of bayonet charges. Then the sacks vanished and were replaced by human beings, including myself, receiving the thrusts of the bayonets. I had enlisted in the medical corp and was baffled at finding myself here. I resolved to resist any attempt to coerce me into the infantry. I would not go on parade after breakfast. Strangely, no one looked for me, and I concealed myself in the long grass of the paddock surrounding our huts. In the balmy fragrance of the earth and the lines of Shakespeare and Virgil, I left my crippling fears.

We newcomers quickly understood we should take any grievances to the camp padre, who was sympathetic and influential. In the pulpit he waxed eloquent, and I shared his passion for language. I was interminably arguing with myself over the existence or non-existence of god, but I loved listening to his sermons and would join the congregation of any church for the sake of hearing the preacher.

The Congregational Church was the most congenial to

my frame of mind, it seemed more concerned with ethics than faith. Clergymen seemed the only beings who remained human in wartime, the only ones who spoke of love, and who acted with love towards others. On Sunday evenings I cut across the dry paddocks into town, to the solid brick church. I followed the sermon carefully, looking for sanction for my pacifist views. After church I joined the supper in the neighbouring hall, and felt compelled to confess my atheist doubts to the ministering girls, which aroused their reserve and even hostility. Yet the aura of the church appealed to me, it was a refuge from the horrors of life outside. The wrought iron fence and gate promised protection, the rising stone facade, a home for my imprisoned feelings. The vacant giant pews provided an uncontested space. Ultimately, the padre got me released from the camp and sent to a hospital ship, moored in Sydney.

I joined the hospital ship tied up at Circular Quay and was quickly infatuated with being aboard the big liner, with little to do and plenty of leave. I congratulated myself on creating this life for myself; philosophy nourished my delusion that I was self-contained. I was now under the authority of women, for the hospital sisters were all lieutenants. The very beings I worshipped were now my enemies. I did not know how to behave. Ignore an officer's orders because she was a woman, or obey them in the spirit of gallantry? The young lieutenants did not like me either, and I soon felt their antagonism growing. I persisted in hiding myself and reading when I should perhaps have been polishing stainless steel. I was never certain what my duties were. The sisters soon sent me to an ambulance corps camp in Wagga.

Banished from the luxurious hospital ship, I could not now escape the chaffing chains of army discipline. Every corporal, even lance-corporal, sergeant, and sergeant major was a god-like master whom I must obey and fear. In the cold of early morning, we marched in fours out through the corrugated iron fence of the showground, a dapper silent lieutenant at our head. Every hour we would squat down for ten minutes, too tired to utter a word.

I went through the motions of being a soldier, but in my imagination I performed those of a lover. I continued to fall in love with every girl I met. At a local dance I met Barbara. Like many country girls she was instinctively a lady, with a regal mien, and restrained composure. Her blue eyes conveyed a deep intelligence. There were more girls sitting demurely against the walls than soldiers willing to dance, which filled me with unexpected courage. Of course, I had no inkling how to dance, but Barbara kept me turning around. We went out into the cold night air and stood by the river. I could think of nothing to say, so I asked her the name of the river. I was disappointed to discover such a narrow river was the famous Murrumbidgee.

I lived two lives at once. My disembodied self was always worshipping an idealised girl, oppressed by my timidity and self-consciousness in her company. Barbara was the first girl of character and intelligence I had met, but I did not have the ability to express my feelings. I had squashed them underfoot too long to be able to respond to the warmth of human beings.

At Wagga I made my first friend in the army. Our tent was beside the show ring. He may have come with me from the hospital ship, for I think the straitlaced sisters would have found him as outlandish as they found me rebellious. He had an ironic cast of mind, which revealed itself in a piquant endearing humour. He was never put out, and would do the most degrading jobs, such as washing the dishes, or cleaning latrines, often with myself, with unruffled good humour. I was bracketed together with him as good for nothing but the most menial tasks. I think he preferred and actually enjoyed doing these, rather than the meaningless, more military tasks. He was even less of a soldier than I was. I could not wholeheartedly return his friendship for my mind was distracted with thoughts of Barbara and sex. As much as I idealised women, I never separated them from sex. They were always sexual beings to me, and sexual intercourse was also an ideal for me. What else could it be, for I had scarcely so much as touched a woman.

I was posted to Armidale and for a while Barbara answered my letters. Soon after, I was put on a boat for New Guinea.

12

Papua New Guinea

The sheer face of the Owen Stanley ranges daunted my longing for freedom. Only in imagination did I see myself slipping through the cracks in its wall. The small hospital under huge marquees was at the entrance to the Kokoda trail. I was condemned to the incessant and debasing drudgery of the ward, sweeping the dirt floor, emptying bottles and pans, and degrading kitchen duties. My heart contracted at again finding myself a menial. Would I ever be free of it? But there was a freedom of sorts. We spread our groundsheets on the earth, and strung our mosquito nets from the tent roof. Everything was on a grand scale, the towering mountains, the unfathomable sky, and the prolific earth. The earth bespoke freedom, but man demanded subservience. Rebellion revolved in my breast, but circumstances choked it.

My guilt found a home in my non-combatancy. Conditioned by my English schooling to be a loyal soldier and a willing sacrifice, and to consider myself a man only when I could fight and kill other men, or be killed by them, I felt I was still a boy, and so I was treated. I envied the men fighting a short distance away and the wounded being brought back to hospital. They were heroes, and I was a renegade. With other orderlies, I competed in searching the heap of their discarded uniforms for their belts and jungle greens, which we wore with puerile conceit.

There were two scrub typhus victims in the ward when I arrived there. Typhus was picked up in the jungle and was thought fatal. One boy, his chest naked, was propped up in the bed like a god. Day after day he remained there, motionless, ministered to exclusively by the sisters, who sequestered any critical event to themselves as though afraid of the true price of war becoming known to the ranks. After a few days of total silence and immobility, he died, and disappeared behind a white screen, through which I was forbidden to go. The other victim lay emaciated and passive like a child, flat on his bed under a sheet. Miraculously, he recovered, the blood returned to his face and he began to move as if in answer to my unspoken prayers. I felt this as a personal success, although my only duty was plying him with endless mugs of cold Ovaltine.

The Japanese bombers throbbed overhead in the milky searchlight. We heard explosions on the distant airfield and the flak of shells would fall around us. Searching as ever for an avenue of escape, I came upon the fragments of an exploded bomber, scattered over a vast area. What was it like to be blown to bits? The pieces were no bigger than leaves.

In the open marquee, which was the mess, a slight young man with a pale angelic face sat stiffly at an upright piano. I sat at the stained trestle table, leaning over my food to disguise my listening. Outside was the brilliant balmy air of the tropics, the imprisoning menace of the jungle and mountains. He was playing a Beethoven sonata. Protracting my lunchtime, I was liberated by dreams of freedom and love. I wanted to speak to the pianist but his expression stopped me, and leaving the marquee, the oppression of war again closed in.

I was transferred to a small signals unit, whose men were kind and easygoing, but still could not assuage my inveterate loneliness. Their attempts to include me in their games and jaunts only stirred more deeply my fears. The tall fatherly sergeant whose bent figure and lean tanned face expressed affection could not eradicate my obsessive horror of authority. He taught us morse code in the long wooden hut, deep in a cutting of the hillside.

The men of the signals unit were seafaring men of free spirit. One half of our long narrow hut was a tangle of baffling wireless equipment, controlled by two omniscient technicians who were deftly discovering a miraculous trail that enabled us to transmit and receive signals from all round the coast of New Guinea. I was afraid of these two for their sinister knowledge. My adoptive father had overborne me with his seemingly intimate knowledge of wireless. Our sergeant had a personality I envied. He was always first when it came to girls. I was still reading Nietzsche and thinking of myself as an undiscovered superman.

A rock strewn hill covered with scorched grass overlooked the spacious bay of the harbour. The army education service was broadcasting a recording of Beethoven's ninth symphony and the cool breath of the water wafted over us where we were seated close together on the ground. It was night and the stars showed through the trees, the velvety darkness warm with the promise of love and humanity, as we waited for the music, the greatest of music, Beethoven. More and more shadows joined the group, squatting down with a hushed joke. I felt the hard earth with my bones, but could make out nothing in the blackness. It was as though our bodies did not exist.

The music began and sailed over the night. Everyone was silent and still. The love I needed seemed to rise up within me, and those I needed to love seemed to be all around me. The great wings of song carried me around the whole earth, revealing the infinite numbers of men to be loved. But the strength and passion all came from within my own heart, crowing and expanding, exploring and owning, with the inrush of its food. The pause between movements was like waiting for love between man to be reborn, and the end, thrusting into the future, was the so urgently wanted love. The night came back to emphasise its utter darkness. Transmuted to spirit, we left the earth unbound from time and space.

Yet, in the daylight, every man was again a familiar, terrifying figure, every face terrible. Craving to be accepted, I could not yield to the replicas of myself that I had learned to hate in my adoptive father. I waited on their transformation into ideal beings, heralded in Beethoven's music and Plato's dialogues. I could not become involved in the making of plonk, or the playing of poker. I remained on the margin, a fastidious spectator.

I was sent in a landing craft to a small wireless station west of Port Moresby on the bank of a deep rapid river where crocodiles lived. All around were swamps and jungle so that the nights teemed with mosquitoes. This river supplied the highlands with food and small craft went repeatedly up and down. It was also the home of many native villages, and we used to see the children romping in the water, their laughter not in the least subdued by the thought of crocodiles. I was to assist a signaller called Gurney already operating the station, which was a wire-screened hut.

In the tropics the vegetation rises up like a wave and dashes itself into one's senses. The jungle is ever new, the rivers are impetuous and laden with mountain soil. I felt naked as though all my arid hypocrisies had released their grip and I was defenceless among primal forces, including that of my real self. I saw myself as one of the wild men who suddenly materialise out of the blank green and black wall of the jungle. Of course, I was afraid of wild men, of my own wildness and its unpredictable consequences.

My hunger for sexual experience drove me to explore the native village. In a clearing, on impacted mud, several native houses rested on high poles. Far reaching branches with sparse foliage rained muted sunlight and shadow over the secluded scene. The village seemed empty but I felt the presence of human beings. I had the naive hope of finding a native girl to love. I knocked respectfully on the wall of the chief's house, which had been described to me. The chief sat on a low bed covered with army blankets while a younger man made me a tin mug of hot strong tea. I knew the stories of the bartering that the white men carried on with natives here; this chief was notorious for it. I had seen him approaching our station on the dirt road from the river, ambling at the head of a group of women and girls of all ages. He left them in the gardens while he came on alone, a look of disarming innocence on his face, magical objects concealed in his heavy clothing. He was very short but disconcertingly powerful. I was afraid to confront him although I wanted very much to get something exotic.

The chief showed me his wares but I had nothing to buy them with and he seemed disinclined to give me anything. I began to feel the same inadequacy I felt before my own people. He could not see I was a black man like himself. I felt he was loathe to talk, or rather, that he was habitually a silent man. I realized I was still looking for my mother and her love, out of the invisible but insuperable bars of the army, into the jungle and its dark people, instinctively feeling a response in their hearts to my own inarticulate paralysed longing.

As I walked away I saw the two girls in the creek. Fear of reprisals by their fathers, and white civilisation's taboo, walled up my desire and I continued on my way like a beaten servant who has coveted the pleasures of his master, conjuring in imagination the revelation of beauty as the girls undressed by the water. I returned penitently to the values of science and imperialism.

One day Gurney took me down the river to visit a priest whose mission stood on a rocky island in the wide estuary. The long-cloaked priest took me back to the gilded sanctuary of my childhood, where I had sold my soul for protection from a barbarous suburban world. But I had turned away from its mirage of peace, and I felt like a guilty boy under the surveillance of the smiling, bland countenance above the ring-like collar. All the time I was on the island I felt him exploring me with the daggers of his kindly eyes. Away from the verandah of the wooden house I examined some of the exercise books the little children thrust proudly up to me. They were proud of learning the white man's language, and the white man's religion — learning to be like white children. I pretended to be impressed, but inwardly felt the loss of something I was trying to grasp, a treasure in this jungle of natural man.

On the way home, we wandered up narrow waterways in the jungle of bristling palms, whose leaves were daggers, crossed to keep inviolate a mysterious interior. All my suppressed terrors and forgotten horrors threatened to find outward shape in these lonely silent parts. The evil black man of the story book haunted the heavy shadows. My companion Gurney, dauntless at the helm of the little boat, continued our hushed intrusion into these silent veins of the jungle while I became petrified with dreams of being permanently immured. Eventually, Gurney turned the boat around and we regained the broad impatient breast of the river, against whose stream we plodded slowly home.

Have I forgotten the terror and suffocation of that loneliness? No, it remains the source of my dreams. For months, years, I was a living person in the iron coffin of war. Slowly dying, I was trying to send a signal through its impassive walls. Everyone else's identity was proven, confirmed by the exclamation of a name and the receipt of a letter, while my own decayed and disappeared in the silence. I entered the desolation of Buna on the back of a truck with other green-clad stragglers from the airfield. The palm trees of the coconut plantations were decapitated, their headless trunks stuck up like poles from the ravished earth. Emasculated and ridiculous, the stumps would never bear fruit again. Rooms were dug out of the earth, covered by logs from coconut palms. These had been torn open, the logs thrown askew, their interiors jagged holes haunted by unknown ghosts. We travelled the subdued road beside the narrow beach and the infinite margin of sea. As we approached headquarters, massive grey wharves, like stages, stood waiting in the sea and, further out, the hulks of liberty ships stood watching, motionless on the sleeping ocean.

Two army tents facing the sea were our wireless station. A tall West Australian and a tubby Victorian were there, both very friendly and tolerant of my ignorance and inexperience of wireless. I was only just beginning to acquire some speed at sending and receiving Morse. I envied the way the Victorian boy accepted and solved every problem, without any pretension to authority.

Behind us, the jungle began, holding up permanent masses of cloud in the distance. The beautiful blue and white billows seemed to laze upon the mountain tops all day. A sandy road led into the jungle, past a grave bearing a cross and a helmet. On the narrow beach, I found a bombed and beached ship, its steel sides and deck rusted, its portholes melted into glass nuggets. I often returned to the ship and loitered among its debris, looking in vain for some small memento of a living being.

The bombers — the flying fortresses — were starting to go overhead in ever-increasing droves towards the Philippines. They would fly low over our tents in the early morning, wing-to-wing, hiding the sky, then straggle back in twos and threes. Occasionally the throb of Japanese planes, returning the visit, would bring us out to search the sky for their elusive formations, suddenly revealed in a beam of searchlight. Then the anti-aircraft gun near us would explode, as the beautiful formation continued sublimely on its way, beyond the reach of all the consternation and terror it was causing on earth.

My whole mind was now obsessed with going on leave. The history in which I was living was a meaningless confining structure. Daydreams of promiscuous romance occupied my thoughts, along with bitterness of heart at the tardiness of invisible authority in granting my leave. The great hulks of the liberty ships stood invitingly out to sea. We would row out to them to watch films on deck, where I envied the domesticity of the American soldiers, even in that outlandish place. They seemed to carry their mothers and sisters and wives with them, by some magic of their perennial childhood.

I did not know then I was longing for my future, that my loneliness was developing my future, delineating the girl whom I should love and marry, and that with that future realised, what gave it birth, the lonely past, would recede into a nightmare. Men have nothing of their own. They unfold nature like other material things. Who can see what aspect of nature it is his lot to unfold? We wait upon the material phenomenon of life to develop before our eyes. We cannot explain it with its own abstract terms. We dare not admit our helplessness even to ourselves.

I was sent from Buna to Salamaua where an army tent stood on the sand beside a magnificent bay of crystal clear water. Salamaua was of recent renown for the valour of the Australian attack that defeated the determined hold of the Japanese. Behind us rose the jungle-covered hills with their mountains of cloud, where in imagination, I could see our soldiers doggedly pursuing the Japanese.

On the other side of the bay the Papuans were holding a festival. A boat filled up with soldiers and crossed the bay and we clambered up over the rocks to the shade of the slender palms. The shining bodies of boys and girls sauntered along the promontory, past the cemetery of war dead, flowers in their hair, and smiles on their faces. The unassuming girls inspired real affection in me for the first time, though I did not try to approach. They were too happy for me, and seemed impregnably protected by their brothers. I sat against the hollow of a weeping gum and contemplated the waveless sea and neat white crosses until the boat returned.

I was finally granted my fortnight's annual leave. I climbed on board a merchant ship and, sleeping anywhere on the cluttered deck, eventually reached Sydney. I shared a room in the Services' Club in Macleay Street, which was packed with soldiers, sailors and airmen who milled about all day in the lounge, waited on by tall, graceful young women. The air was stuffy with the smell of uniforms and brilliantine. I hung about the streets of the city, haunting cafes and bookshops, before I was sent to a family who had offered their hospitality to a soldier.

I walked between the opulent gardens of solid houses to the street where Mr and Mrs Gorsky lived. Mrs Gorsky embodied my few romantic intimations of Asiatic beauty. Small, slender, with coarse black hair and milk-white skin, she dressed elegantly, her hair in perfect turns upon her head. She was a universal person, an eloquent humanist. Yet in spite of her genial temperament, I felt suspicion and this was fed by her husband's disconcerting diffidence. His unflickering gaze exposed my own unsureness of myself, my lack of principle, of loyalties; my watery will which might yield before any mischief. He had the businessman's scent for irresponsibility. I had no purpose in his richly appointed home but to scavenge. He knew I would fall in love with his wife and covet her. But there was no need for him to worry. His middle-class culture inexorably separated me from her, and from his beautiful daughter.

Mrs Gorsky was fond of remembering her Russian

education. She was proud of the enlightenment she had received from its teaching of comparative religion, and reproached our schools for their narrowness. She was a mysterious woman, old enough to be my mother, with whom I could fall platonically in love. But her daughter aroused only my sexual desires. Ada was terribly alluring to me with her mixture of Australian candour and eastern beauty. Her demeanour was totally egalitarian. I could not overcome my timorous nature with her though. She was a wealthy man's daughter. I was in my own prison. All night long, sleeping in a makeshift bed next to Ada's bedroom, I tossed and turned with the riddle of how to approach this beautiful young woman. Her door was open and I sat on the edge of my bed, torn between passion and cowardly resignation. Perhaps it was my want of a real father that had left me without assertiveness or resourcefulness.

I shrank from the prospect of returning to New Guinea, and puzzled over ways of escape. Down in the basement of the Services' Club I threw my pass-book into the flames of the boiler, but this gave me only a few days before I was issued a new one.

This time, I was sent to Lae. My mind became obsessed by delusions of escape. At one end of the road was the sea, where I saw the idle liberty ships waiting for me; at the other was the air strip, where the flying fortress with its freedom-loving American crew was roaring in expectation of my arrival. I no longer thought of the jungle as a sanctuary. Its immeasurable ebullience and fecundity made it alien. I had to get back to civilisation and women. On one of my long walks through Lae I wandered into an airfield of fighter planes. A large plane was being checked out on the field; it was full of Americans going on leave in Australia. I wanted to make a dash for it and throw myself on their generosity.

I went into the American canteen. I felt much freer among the Americans. Their generous and genial natures attracted me, although I had heard of their merciless behaviour towards their black soldiers. I joined the packed counter, wondering if I would get a cup of tea, being a foreigner, but I was given one without question, and wound my way to a place by myself among the close tables, where long-legged airmen lounged. Two tall black men joined me and began talking to me in an engaging way. They were beautiful beings, not just physically, but in their nature, and I felt unusually at ease with them. They spoke to me as a father might speak to his son, inviting me to their hut, which was alongside the airstrip. It was like a dormitory, very neatly and cleanly kept. Several men were lying on their beds, reading or talking. My two companions showed me photographs of naked men and women in sexual intercourse. I rather liked them, especially the beautiful bodies of the women, but my enjoyment was short-lived. A soldier at the far end of the hut signalled to my companions with a mute but eloquent rebuke, to send me away.

Our officer had not come with our small signals unit and I wandered about aimlessly, unable to escape the influence of the explosive jungle that towered over our small human eruption. All the time it tempted me with a freedom that I did not know how to take. I felt guilty and divested of responsibility as badly wounded men were brought in from the cloaking jungle to the newly erected canvas hospital.

We small group of signallers were in one army tent that

stood open towards the still sea. Our camp stretchers stood end to end and there was nothing one could do without being critically observed. The island was too small to find privacy anywhere. Day after day, our wireless equipment and debonair lieutenant failed to arrive. I sat on the edge of my camp stretcher, exposed under an inner burden of loneliness, alienation, and pain. A heritage perhaps of my heavy farm work, my ego evaporated several hours every day in abdominal pain, whose cause was obscure to me. The pain demoralised me, and intensified my reserve in the presence of my companions. The silence between us oppressed me and the sound of their voices terrified me. They spoke to one another in simple statements, as though out of an elementary school text book, each dogmatic statement rebuffed by another, and a victorious laugh. I could not catch on to this way of passing on the wasted hours, and lay on my bunk, listening intently. Yet, I liked them, and felt that they liked me; the solid, short boy from Fitzroy, untiringly recounting the same football matches; the tall god-like figure of the boy from Perth, who would listen patiently to the tales of football, and add commentaries here and there with a winning smile. One could easily imagine his bright young brothers, beautiful sisters, and loving mother and father. There was an older man, our mechanic, hard as iron outside, but solid gold inside. He had little ones of his own, and showed towards me an inclination towards fatherliness, so I savoured the conviction he was my friend. We seemed to recognise one another as inhabitants of alien worlds. Like many practical people, he appreciated the world of words, while he knew I admired machines and the way, like Vulcan, he had them in the palm of his hand. Behind the hessian of the shower,

I used to admire and envy his fully developed form, ashamed of my own puny growth.

At length, bewildered by my physical discomfort, I went on sick parade and joined the line of soldiers who one by one entered the doctor's tent. We were all bent in introspection, wondering whether our pains were real or imaginary. Somehow you had to prove they were not imaginary, for the medical world assumed everybody was seducing them, as though every soldier was a consummate actor. I began to doubt whether I was not deceived by an ulterior desire to escape the tedium and drudgery of life on the island. Apparently there was a physical source to my pain, though, for the doctor sent me to hospital on the mainland for a minor operation.

The hospital was large, with marquees clustered together under the wall of the jungle, their steep canvas roofs almost touching one another. There is something sublime about the infant-like surrender of wounded men, but their drained faces stirred guilt in my soul for my non-participation. I felt at home in the hospital grounds and the nightmare of starting over again the barren life on the island was never absent from my mind. I enjoyed watching the attention and treatment the wounded received from the solicitous orderlies. Male nurses seemed to be even more compassionate and understanding of the men's needs than the sisters, and they were all privates like myself. I was allowed to wander freely around the hospital, in what seemed to be an unusual absence of authority. I wanted to lengthen my time in this agreeable place as long as possible and an attack of malaria enabled me to do so.

Coming unexpectedly on a bottle of sleeping pills on my solitary tour of the ward, I furtively unscrewed the top and poured out a handful. I swallowed them. Lying in bed, I eventually felt them working. Next, I blurringly heard people arguing beside my bed. They were trying to work out how many pills I had swallowed, and seemed to be overestimating the number. I sank into a lassitude. It was gratifying to hear the concern for me in the voices of the orderlies and doctors, although one doctor thought I was shamming and spoke about sticking pins in me. Indeed, I did dully feel them being stuck in my feet, but my limbs did not stir. Eventually, I was aware of a soft voice speaking to me. Opening my eyes I saw the lean, lined face of a cultivated Englishman sitting on a hard chair beside me, bent over some papers. He began to question me about my childhood. He was interested and keenly curious. I enjoyed telling him all I could recall about my past, and on reflection, it seemed a sorry story.

Late at night the ambulance drew up outside a fenced-in hut. It was pitch dark and profoundly silent. The cage-like gates were opened and we were smuggled in by the grumbling orderlies, although they treated us patients kindly. I was separated from the others and led down a corridor to a narrow door where I was left alone in a large room, empty but for a low bed with a grey blanket. The door was shut and bolted. I sat on the edge of the bed, assailed by the tangible darkness, unable to see my fate, and becoming aware of an overpowering scent which I recognised intuitively as the smell of madness. I knew it threatened my very reason, my distance from events. I lay down but could not sleep in the heavy ominous silence. As dawn invaded my room a terrible clamour arose from the corridor. There was indeed a raving madman close by. Once his cries had begun they did not cease all day, shouts of terrible anger, rolling out one after another. I stayed isolated until I saw the doctor, listening to the demented cries and breathing the horrible smell. At length, I was let out, and walking down the corridor saw three cages, in one of which was the source of the demon-like cries. His contorted countenance and explosive movements struck me with terror. On the other side of the corridor in a large wire netting enclosure several men seemed to be skylarking. One of them looked at me with such hatred and contempt, I cringed before his gaze. My memory was indelibly impressed with the ravaged contours of his face, which seemed to have been gouged out by some diabolic hand. There was an unnerving laugh in his sunken eyes. He raised his fists at me and I was back on the verandah at Fairbridge Farm, shrinking under the blows of triumphant boys.

 I continued down the corridor into a large dining room where I found a collection of men who treated me with disinterested kindness. They were all going to be writers and artists. I had never met such people before. I was elated to meet a real writer, but I soon discovered that this writing did not go far beyond the idea of writing, and so with the others. I was in the nebulous world of unrealisable ideas, of men led by impractical dreams. But they were generous and gentle companions, with self-effacing smiles, or profound expressions of self always on their faces. And the doctor, whom I saw in his office, was not unlike his patients. Sublime acceptance seemed expressed in his long, lined face. His voice was seductive and low and to my relief and surprise, he assured me I was being sent home.

13

A Vision of a Kinder World

On leaving the army in Sydney, I was given a job in the Public Service, and recommended to a doctor, but I had nowhere to live. I liked the warmth of the big city. An estate agent in the Cross got me a cellar in Macleay Street, with bare brick walls and damp floor. I felt lost and lonely and despaired my want of purpose and presence of mind.

I visited the doctor assigned to me by the army. He spoke to me as an equal, making me more embarrassed than ever. He invited me to come to dinner at his home and introduced me to his daughter who radiated the kind of sympathy I craved, but hoped for in vain, for she was educated and wealthy. The doctor was an evangelist, and abjured me to adopt a love of god as a remedy for my despair. He gave me an introduction to the Oxford Group, who had an office in the city. Here I met a missionary family from the islands of the north. How privileged they seemed, and exempt from the common worries of the world. No one can see an individual's birthright, and the way he has been oppressed since birth.

My job was in a big barn of an office in Harrington

Street, supervising a company of land army girls still in uniform and fresh from their country life, seated at little desks in pairs like a class of schoolgirls, sorting boxes of cards whose content I never understood. The girls saw themselves when looking at me. We were reflections of one another, uneducated, innocent young people, expecting the ideal to materialise. They sensed I was a farm labourer like themselves. Supervising was foreign and odious to me. The girls were more intelligent than we three uncomfortably trousered animals watching them. I was especially fond of a tall fair girl who seemed to be the leader of the group, although her rosy complexion, her slim erect figure, her coil of wheaten hair were rendered bitter by her supercilious mien. But lust kept fermenting daydreams and ephemeral hopes. Not one of the girls seemed interested in me or volunteered to dispel my chronic loneliness, which sank me further into self-contempt.

I would walk out into the chill walls of the city, and climb the flights of concrete steps to the bridge. Every girl who approached was the answer to my prayer, but my pleading gaze into their eyes met no response. Every man approaching with impatient steps was a threat that stirred memories of first fights and filled me with cowardly tears.

I moved from the city to North Sydney. From the large sash window of my room, I looked down upon the cobblestones of the backyard. An impoverished family occupied a lean-to wooden dwelling down the side of the yard. Half-clad children played noisily in the grime and mud. Parents shouted violently at one another. I was terrified of them all, although I loved watching the children.

I loved walking over the bridge to work, floating

between sea and sky. I loved the rock-like pylons, like witnesses of some ancient, inexpressible myth. But the people walked by in icy spheres and I never once exchanged a word with anyone.

I was transferred to the pharmaceutical department. I sat all day lifting one prescription after another out of a long narrow box, and ticking it off on typed sheets that reached me monotonously from the army of typists in their vast chamber across the corridor. At lunchtime I would gravitate down the wide granite steps to Wynyard Park, and sit on the grass staring enviously at the happy couples. The war was over: love and friendship were freed from the menace of separation and death.

Next to Wynyard Station was Tyrell's dimly lit second-hand bookshop. It was a cage of refuge and hope. Mr Tyrell haunted the aisles like a shadow. I sensed his contempt for such a slave of the written word as I and longed to raise myself in his esteem.

I seemed to be in unrelenting confrontation with humanity, in which I always retreated vanquished. Every man was a potential attacker, about to accost me.

But my life was imperceptibly changing. In the Cross I sat on the balcony of the Arabian Coffee Lounge, overlooking the feverish life of Darlinghurst Road. A handsome man and woman, two actors from the nearby Minerva Theatre, must have felt my loneliness, and with beautiful smiles, spoke to me, enquiring what I wanted to be. I answered I was going to be a poet, but looking at me intently, they prophesied that I would be a painter. The warmth of their presence evoked in me a vision of a kinder more affectionate world where no one was lonely and unloved. Their love for each other spread around them.

I had always despised my uneducated state and thought I could accomplish nothing without a degree. Every poet and writer seemed to have been to university, and I felt they owed their eminence to this. I got my back pay from the army and it was enough to live on without a job for a year, so I decided to try to matriculate and realise my ideal of attending a university, there being free places available for returned soldiers.

I found a small room on the high road above Balmoral Beach, let to me by a war widow still wrapped in her grief, who had a very loving and precocious son of about ten. They both suffered uncomplainingly the injustice of the world, the boy making valiant efforts to take the place of his father and protect his mother. I had a tiny verandah room while another large room was let to a family with a young child. I had never seen a whole family living in one room before.

I was finally free to choose my own path, and this helped my self-esteem. But still I remained painfully shy. The ten-year-old boy inhibited me with his assurance.

Mr Cornforth was a matriculation coach whose home was in an idyllic spot just above the sands of Balmoral. A band of young people, largely from wealthy families, came to him to do the matriculation privately. The dozen boys and girls of between sixteen and twenty were all very handsome. I was twenty-six. It was twelve years since I left school. I felt simple and clumsy, and close to tears much of the day. At lunchtime we used to go down to the beach. The young boys would take their suit jackets off but I was too shy to remove mine and would swelter in the heat. Some of the girls would lie in their swimming costumes to get a tan. One girl was exquisitely proportioned; her flesh as smooth and firm as the sky. My efforts to engage her interest met with a contemptuous response and, learning by muttered remarks that she was of a very wealthy family, I accepted the futility of my desires. But I could not stop my fascination with her shape or imagining an idyllic life with her.

Somehow I matriculated, and in 1947 I enrolled at Sydney University. In the dark, narrow lecture room the superficial world was shut out.

Epilogue

Lionel Pearce died while this book was still in production. He had written a long and emotive manuscript that finished abruptly just after his return from the Second World War, when he was in his mid-twenties. He did not want to write about the rest of his life. For him, writing was a process of trying to deal with the effects of a painful and traumatic childhood.

What follows was the result of an interview with Lionel recorded by his daughter Alexandra following a request for a final chapter that could lend the work a better sense of completion. He was quite frail at this time.

I enjoyed attending lectures at the university, the accommodating atmosphere, working out problems in science together. In my second year there I met the girl who became my wife; she was an art student, studying at East Sydney Tech. Later I taught zoology and botany. My wife and I had a large family, and some of my happiest moments were spent watching the children, each so different from the other, playing together harmoniously. I took them on long hikes in the bush, in the steep gorges of the Dividing Ranges.

But through all the years I could never forget the sorrows of my early life. I think people always saw me as unhappy, and I think that fundamentally I was, all my life. I am still grieving for my mother. I never believed she was dead. A reserve has always separated me from other people. I feel this life I am leading is not my real life. That is in the north of England, with my mother. One day I will get back to it.